PICKLEHEAD

'I'm not going to tell the story the way it happened. I'm going to tell it the way I remember it.'

DAVID MAMET

Rohan Candappa
PICKLEHEAD

*From Ceylon to suburbia; a memoir of food,
family and finding yourself*

EBURY
PRESS

First published in Great Britain 2006

1 3 5 7 9 10 8 6 4 2

Text © Rohan Candappa 2006

Rohan Candappa has asserted his right to be identified as the author
of this work under the Copyright, Designs and Patents Act 1988.

Ebury Press, an imprint of Ebury Publishing.
Random House, 20 Vauxhall Bridge Road, London SW1V 2SA

Random House Australia (Pty) Limited
20 Alfred Street, Milsons Point, Sydney,
New South Wales 2061, Australia

Random House New Zealand Limited
18 Poland Road, Glenfield, Auckland 10, New Zealand

Random House (Pty) Limited
Isle of Houghton, Corner Boundary Road & Carse O'Gowrie,
Houghton, 2198, South Africa

The Random House Group Limited Reg. No. 954009

www.randomhouse.co.uk

A CIP catalogue record for this book is available from the British Library.

Cover design by 2 Associates
Interior by seagulls.net

ISBN 9 780091 897789 (from Jan 2007)
ISBN 0 091 89778 5

Papers used by Ebury Press are natural, recyclable
products made from wood grown in sustainable forests.

Printed and bound in Great Britain by Mackays of Chatham Plc

contents

1	Aisle Seven	1
2	My Name Is	13
3	A Pinch of Salt	15
4	Potato Curry	27
5	The Lookers-In	55
6	Ceylon	73
7	A Mangosteen in the Applee Tree	99
8	P.S. Bring Groom	111
8½	A Brief History of Curry in Britain: Part One	123
9	Fish	135
9½	A Brief History of Curry in Britain: Part Two	159
10	A Swirl of Black	171
10½	A Brief History of Curry in Britain: Part Three	195
11	I Bring You Frankincense	203
12	Two Meals	219
12½	A Brief History of Curry in Britain: Part Four	235
13	The Wine Will Be Flat	247
14	Lentils, Lentils, Everywhere	263
15	Plastic Boxes	273
16	A Curry After Work	287
16½	A Brief History of Curry in Britain: A Postscript	297
17	'The Arena of Food'	305
	Acknowledgements	312
	About the Author	314

PREFACE

I couldn't have written this book without my mother. She told me the stories. All I did was write them down. This book is for her and, of course, for my father. I hope that I have done them some kind of justice.

I also couldn't have written this book without Jan, who is more than my wife, and more than I deserve.

The other people I must thank are Valentine & Ranee Gunesekera and Barbara & Dennis Goonting. Your generosity and love and willingness to share your time and your memories made so much of this book possible.

And the book would have remained nothing more than a dream without the support, encouragement and belief of Hannah MacDonald at Ebury and Simon Trewin at PFD. Thank you.

Finally the book is for my children – so that one day they might understand a little better the fool who is their father. Thank you both for everything you give me. I truly am a lucky man.

Rohan Candappa
DECEMBER 2005

one

AISLE SEVEN

'You're Indian, you'll like this,' said the kindly Irish dinner lady. 'It's curry.'

I considered the proposition. More correctly, I considered the proposition for as long as a ten-year-old schoolboy in short trousers and seriously scuffed Clarks Pathfinder shoes could consider anything when he would rather be outside in the playground continuing the three-playtimes-old game of football which his team was currently losing 74–72.

What should I do?

It was a real dilemma. Even at that early age I realised that some kind of cultural test was being laid before me. For as long as I had been conscious of anything beyond the safe comfort of my family and home, I had known that I was different to the people around me. After all, this was 1970s Britain. A Britain in which Harold Wilson and Ted Heath slugged out a political battle with real ideological differences. Where The Bay City Rollers and Slade divided playgrounds across the land on what seemed to be strictly gender lines. Where the tank-top was regarded an item of high fashion. And where you didn't often come across a South London born and bred (and buttered) Ceylonese-Burmese-Portuguese-Roman Catholic whose dad painted abstract paintings and who, for some unfathomable reason, had decided to support Leeds United – the nation's most hated football team – even though he had never been further north than the number 12 bus would go on a Saturday.

Admittedly there was my brother, but he, somewhat more sensibly, had decided to support Tottenham Hotspur. So obviously we were two completely different people.

'Go on, you'll like it, it's curry.' By now the kindly Irish dinner lady (apparently, back then, kindliness and Irishness were the key criteria for acceptance and advancement in the dinner-lady profession) was proffering a ladle filled with the culinary delight in question.

The problem was that it didn't look like curry. It looked like a ladle of over-stewed grey school mince. With raisins in it.

If there was one thing I had learned from countless meals cooked by my mother and eaten amid the everyday madness of family life, it was that curry never had raisins in it.

Curry had chicken or beef or lamb or mutton or fish or prawns in it. It was alive with the heat of chillies, or the tang of ginger, or the sweetness of coconut, the bite of mustard seeds or the sourness of tamarind. It could be light enough to dance delicately across your tongue, or fierce enough to have your largest uncle mopping perspiration from his brow. And as you ate it you were surrounded by people talking and laughing and listening and telling stories and sharing jokes, and feeling, maybe for just a few moments, the hot sun of a distant land warm up even the most sullen of 1970s English days.

And it never ever had raisins in it.

I was just about to plump for the low-fat spam-fritter-and-chips option, when from behind me a sneering child's voice, which I already knew too well, proffered an obviously well-considered and Oscar Wilde-like jibe.

'Eughh! Smelly curry! Yuk!'

Laughter ricocheted around the dining hall. But every bullet somehow hit home. I could feel myself shrinking and my face reddening.

Clearly the stakes had been raised.

What should I do? Take the 'curry' or go for the spam fritters and chips? It was a very hard decision. But – I am proud to say – I rose to the occasion. Defiantly I lifted my plate, looked straight into the dinner lady's eyes and said, 'Curry, please.'

The dinner lady smiled. The ladle was hoisted. The ladle was tipped. And a sea of over-stewed grey school mince, with raisins in it, spread over the pristine white plate like an oil slick seeping out of a stricken tanker. Half a spoon of rice was added and some over-boiled cabbage. (After all, this was the 1970s and over-boiled cabbage was the closest thing the country's education system had to a national curriculum.)

3

I walked triumphantly back to my table. I knew, I just knew, that the rest of my playground football team would follow my lead. Soon we would all be tucking into our platefuls of what, despite all evidence to the contrary, would no doubt prove to be delicious curry. It would be like that moment right at the end of *Spartacus*. The movie had been on the telly that weekend and it may well have had some bearing on my actions. At the end of the film, Spartacus and his army of freedom-craving slaves had been defeated. As the victorious Roman general walked among the conquered, he asked for the vanquished leader to stand up so that he could be crucified. Kirk Douglas got wearily to his feet and said, 'I am Spartacus.' But then so did the man at his side. And then someone further along. And before you knew it, every one of the hundreds of once despondent slaves covering the hillside were on their feet defiantly bellowing out, 'I am Spartacus.'

Unfortunately the rest of my football team had obviously been watching the other side. They went for the spam fritters and chips. Every single one of them.

To be honest, they'd made the right choice. The 'curry' was awful. It tasted like over-stewed grey school mince with raisins in it. But I ate it anyway.

* * *

Nothing much happened for the next thirty-one years.

Aisle seven of the Harringey branch of Sainsbury's is an odd place to have a moment of self-revelation. But that's where I had mine. It was 11.33 a.m. It was a Wednesday morning. Outside it was raining.

By the time most people start coasting away from their thirties, they pretty much know who they are. I was no different. I had found a way to make a reasonable living. I had a wife I loved. I had children of my own. And I had long since stopped looking in the mirror and wondering who was looking back.

When the moment of revelation came, just like the scene in the school dinner queue all those years ago, it involved curry. All I did was reach out for a 500-gram jar of Sainsbury's own label korma cooking sauce.

I spun the jar round in my hand and read the label.

Cut 500g skinless, boneless chicken breasts into bite-size pieces. Heat 1 tablespoon of oil in a saucepan, add the chicken and cook for 3–4 minutes. Stir in the sauce, cover and simmer gently for 20 minutes, stirring occasionally.

Making a curry was that simple. But there was something about the prospect that made me feel uneasy. And it had nothing to do with what the curry might actually taste like. The longer I stared at the jar, the more the uneasiness simmered.

For me, growing up in 1970s London, my identity had always centred on my family. It wasn't nationality, socio-

6

economic class, religion, neighbourhood, schooling or even ethnicity that would have first come to mind if anyone had ever asked who I was. It would be family. I was my parents' son. My brother's brother. My grandmother's grandchild. And my uncles' and aunts' nephew. Of course, irrevocably tied up in the idea of family were issues of nationality, socio-economic class, religion, neighbourhood, schooling and ethnicity, but family always came first.

In my mind, and in my experience, the idea of family was synonymous with the idea, experience and glorious enjoyment of food. Family and food. You couldn't separate the two. Where there was family, there was food. Where there was food, there was family. And the food wasn't just any old food. There were Sri Lankan chicken curries as red as fire. Burmese noodles drowned in coconut gravy. Deep-fried aubergines and peppers mixed into a salad. Subtle fish molees that stained rice an almost fluorescent yellow. A fear-some vindaloo with chunks of pork the size of children's building blocks. Fish and meat patties spiked with sliced chillies and shaped like half moons. And flat breads. And rice noodles. And pickles. And Asian spiced roasts. And sweets sticky with syrup. And more types of curries than you could eat in a month.

But here was I with a jar in my hand of ready-made, mass-produced, mass-marketed and blandly spiced korma sauce.

I bought the jar anyway. I bought it because it was on the shopping list, and I'd already got the chicken, and I was in a hurry. Also because I knew that the kids would eat it. As their diet usually consisted of chicken nuggets and chips, pesto pasta and McDonald's Happy Meals, I suppose I was trying to kid myself that a chicken korma, even if it came from a jar from Sainsbury's, did, somehow, reflect their cultural background.

By the time I got home, however, I'd had a change of heart. I'd decided to cook a proper chicken curry for them. From scratch. Just like my mother used to make. Just like I'd eaten all those times around the family table. It was something I hadn't done for years. It was something, I realised, that would help me reassert who I truly was.

Unfortunately, when I rang my mum she was out.

In the kitchen on a shelf above the fridge, I have a collection of cookbooks. I tend to go for the ones with large, mouth-watering, colour pictures of whatever it is that you're supposed to be making. This is because most of the time all I do is look at the pictures. Actually cooking the stuff often seems too much like hard work. I will, occasionally, get a book down and leaf through it and pretend that I'm going to use it. But if I do, I'll always end up deciding on the one or two recipes that I've cooked before. The rest of the pages stay ignored and unspattered.

I had just selected *INDIAN COOKING: traditional cuisine with many exotic curries* when the small puddle that was my two children got back from the park. (Why is it that rain doesn't bother children?) I tried to enthuse them for the culinary adventure that lay ahead.

'Hey, kids, we're going to make chicken curry for dinner!'

'Why?'

It was Small Child A who had spoken. It was Small Child B who was looking at me intently to see how I would handle this curve ball.

'Because it's lovely and it's part of your cultural heritage.'

'Can I watch a video?'

This was Small Child B.

'No. We're going to make chicken curry. And we're going to make it together. Proper chicken curry. It'll be fun.'

'Waaaaahhhhh!'

Admittedly Small Child B was only five years old. But all the same his response was just a little disappointing. And anyway this was important.

'It'll be fun! Come on, we can do it together!'

'Where's Tiggy?' Small Child A again.

'Leave Tiggy alone. She's probably having a sleep upstairs on a bed somewhere. Anyway, we're going to be doing coo—'

Exit Small Child A (who's seven and hence in charge of instigating and co-ordinating all household insurrections) followed by Small Child B, off to search for, and no doubt torment, the cat.

'Bloody hell, I'll just make the sodding thing myself then.'

This was Large Dad C. A far from happy Large Dad C.

I turned to page 39 of *INDIAN COOKING: traditional cuisine with many exotic curries*. Murgh ka salan – chicken curry. The picture was very appealing. And reassuringly ethnic. But the recipe called for eighteen ingredients.

I searched the kitchen. I had six of them. One of the six I had was water.

On top of that there was this:

Preparation time: 40 minutes
Cooking time: about 1 hour 20 minutes

I picked up the jar of Sainsbury's korma sauce and checked how long that would take.

Twenty-four minutes versus two hours when you live in a cash-rich but time-poor world really is a bit of a no-brainer. But as I chopped the chicken breast fillets into pieces, fried them in a pan and poured the sauce over them, I knew that, on some intangibly unsettling level, it was a no-culturer too.

If you're the child of immigrant parents, the food you eat at home is more than just the food you eat at home. It is a link to the world your parents came from. It has echoes of past places, past people and past events. It is a conduit of both family history and history in a far wider sense. Sit down at your parents' table and happily help yourself from the dishes they lay out before you, and with every mouthful you eat you are, in fact, doing so much more than just eating.

In the years between the grey school mince with raisins in it and aisle seven of Sainsbury's, I had undoubt-edly lost something. What exactly it was that I had lost, I wasn't sure.

What's even harder to understand is how, over the same period of time that I had drifted away from my culinary heritage, curry had gone from being 'smelly and foreign' to being, according to the late Robin Cook, 'the most popular dish in Britain'. Jars of curry sauce lined whole aisles of supermarkets and ready meals were piled high in chiller cabinets. A curry after work had become as much a part of the employment scene as whingeing about the Christmas party or not knowing how to add toner to the photocopier. And the very word 'vindaloo' had become the central, celebratory refrain of the England football team's World Cup song. So how, exactly, had all this happened?

And what, if any, was the link between what I had lost and what the country had gained?

two
MY NAME IS

So where do I begin?

Write about what you know, that's what they always say.

Well, this much I know. My name is Rohan Candappa. I live in North London with my wife, two children, two cats and a mortgage.

I was born forty-mumble-mumble years ago in South London. I went to school in East Dulwich. I went to university in Reading. Then I blagged my way into advertising and didn't get found out for almost twenty years.

Now I write books. Mainly small books. Small humorous books. The problem with writing humorous books is that no one takes you seriously. But then again, what can you expect, you write humorous books.

My mother is of Portuguese descent, was born in Burma, escaped to India during the Second World War, then came to England in the 1950s where she met my father. He came from Ceylon and had come to London to become an architect. He also painted abstract paintings. And that's enough about my parents to be going on with. To be honest, it's about as much as I knew all the time that I was growing up.

three

A PINCH OF SALT

In November 1728 the *São Gabriel* was sailing towards Cochin on the west coast of India. It had been at sea for nine months. Months that had worked the Portuguese sailors mercilessly and had hardened their muscles and tightened their skins. But it had been a good voyage. Only two dead. Both through accidents. No major sickness on board. And the storms of the Cape of Good Hope had been navigated with only minor damage.

The crew were in good heart. Ahead of them in Cochin lay the prospect of unloading the cargo of Portuguese goods that were stacked in caskets, bales and barrels below deck. Then spices would be reloaded that would fill the holds with the aromas of the still new and exotic world that many aboard would be encountering for the first time. Back in Lisbon, the spices would make both the captain of the ship and the merchants who had financed the voyage into wealthy men. Or wealthier men, in the case of the merchants. Of course, very little of the profit would trickle down to the sailors. They were just hired hands. Happy to be working. And lucky to return home in one piece with enough money in their pockets to see them through the lean times when no ships were in sight that needed a crew. Their money would also be handed over to the families they had left at home, as the majority of the crew were devout Catholics who would, on their return, gather their wives and children and give thanks in the local church.

In Cochin, in between the unloading and reloading, the crew would have time off in the port. Time to stretch their legs, time to feel the assurance of solid land under their feet, time to go to church, and time to eat, drink and be merry. And after so many long months at sea, the simple pleasures of at last eating fresh meat and fruit and vegetables, and seeing faces other than those of your crewmates, were not to be underestimated. No wonder, as they approached the safety of the harbour, that spirits were high.

The storm, when it hit, came out of nowhere.

The first sign was a quickening of the wind from the west. But no one took much notice of it. Land was in sight and the prospect of much-longed-for time ashore beckoned. It was early evening and the crew were eating what passed for a meal for these, by now, sea-hardened veterans. But the wind kept blowing. Clouds raced in to smother out the last embers of the setting sun. Dusk, short-lived, had been snatched away and now darkness embraced the ship as it rode the mounting waves. Amidst urgent shouts meals were abandoned, loose fittings tied down, and sails hurriedly furled up and lashed tightly to the cross spars of the mast.

Now the rain came. First vertically. Then diagonally. Then horizontally. Rain that drilled into the sailors like falling arrows and then, as the storm built, like volleys of crossbow bolts, finally hitting them full in the face like a hail of musket balls.

All sailors, back then, knew about storms. They knew what to do. They knew where to go. They knew what to loosen, what to tie down and what to throw overboard. So while their shouts grew ever louder against the howling wind, there was no panic. But there was fear. Because they all knew that every storm held within it the possibility of their death. And the death of everyone aboard the ship. And it is a foolish sailor who does not fear the sea, or the sea's capricious mistress, the weather.

Stand firm, hold to your tasks, use every ounce of strength that you possess, and, God willing, you will survive. As the storm built, as the sea raged, prayers to a most merciful deity were on the lips of every sailor, from the captain down.

But God's mind must have been elsewhere.

Even in the cacophonous howling of the gale, the snap of the mast as it broke in two could be heard. It could be heard as clearly as the tolling of church bells announcing yet another funeral, on a sleepy day, in the sun-drenched hills of the small towns in southern Portugal, where many of the sailors had come from. Maybe as the water closed around

17

them their minds flew back across oceans and continents and they saw again their homes, their wives, their children, all smiling in the midday brilliance at their return. And maybe as the salt water filled their mouths, and their lungs, and their eyes, they prayed to a God that had forsaken them to at least protect the ones they loved.

Two men survived the shipwreck. Washed ashore on the island of Vypeen, off the coast of Cochin. They were found the next morning, collapsed on the beach, barely alive. Around them, scattered across the golden sands, lay the splintered timbers and smashed cargo that was all that was left of the *São Gabriel*.

One of the men was Antonio Fernandez. The other was Francisco Rebello. Francisco Rebello was my great-great-great-great-great-grandfather.

Unfortunately, much of the tale I've just recounted is made up. I blame it all on the fact that I've spent too many Sunday evenings watching *Time Team* on Channel 4. That's the show where archaeologists recreate the lifestyle of a whole ancient settlement from little more than a fragment of a rim of a bowl dug up in a back garden.

In my case, the fragment of the rim of a bowl was the name Francisco Rebello. He was my ancestor. And he was reputed to have been shipwrecked off the coast of Cochin some time in the 1700s. But beyond these two slivers of information there is no evidence of what actually happened.

So my version of things might be true. It's just that it probably isn't. But then again aren't all histories, to a certain extent, fictions?

Look up Vypeen in travel guides today and you will discover very little. The Lonely Planet book tells you that you can get to the island by ferry from Fort Cochin. And that there are: '… miles of surf beaches but bathers will feel most comfortable at Cherai Beach, 35km from the ferry, where there are a couple of basic cafés and guesthouses. The island also boasts a lighthouse, good beaches and the early 16th-century Pallipuran Fort (open Thursday).' While the only mention the Rough Guide makes of Vypeen is as part of the directions on how to get to Cherai Beach.

For me, however, Vypeen is a sort of ancestral home. Generations of my mother's family were born and grew up on the island. My Catholic faith, before I wandered away from it as an adolescent, had its roots there. And the island lives on for me in stories my mother tells, and recipes that my family cooks.

Vypeen has no great place in the history of the world. But it was on the periphery of a place that did change the globe. That's because Fort Cochin, believed by some to be the oldest European settlement in India, was just a short boat ride away.

It all started in 1494 when Pope Alexander VI did that most papal thing of dividing the then supposedly 'undiscovered' world into two halves. Spain was given the world west of the Atlantic. Portugal had first dibs on everything to the east. As a result, the Portuguese were the first Europeans to discover the sea route to India, and in 1498 the twenty-eight-year-old Vasco da Gama landed at Calicut, a port 85 miles up the coast from Cochin.

Some accounts state that when Vasco reached Calicut he found a harbour with 700 ships tied up. Clearly, it was the major port from which the Moors controlled the spice routes out of India. As such, it was unlikely that the Portuguese would have found it easy to set up shop. At Cochin, however, a far smaller port not dominated by the Moors, they would have been made more welcome. Hence Cochin's claim to be the oldest European settlement in India. Before long the Portuguese switched their focus to Calicut, but for a brief period Cochin was the key location.

Indeed, on Christmas Eve in 1524 Vasco da Gama, on a return trip to India, died in Cochin. He was buried in the church where his body remained for fourteen years before it was returned to Portugal.

The next date of real note was 1663, when the Dutch arrived. Although 'arrived' is probably too polite a word for what happened. One of their first acts was to order all European Catholic priests to leave their territory, then they destroyed all the churches and convents they could find. The only one they spared was the Cochin church dedicated to St Antony, which they stripped of its finery and converted to an austere Dutch Protestant ministry.

But the Dutch were not totally unreasonable masters. Realising that there were a large number of Portuguese and Portuguese-descended people living in the colony, they allowed the gilded screen from the church to be taken from

St Antony's in Cochin to the island of Vypeen and installed in a more modest Catholic church there.

As a result Vypeen rapidly became the stronghold of the area's Portuguese community. Which probably explains how my mother's ancestors ended up there.

A hundred and thirty years on from the Dutch takeover, the British 'arrived' in Cochin. So by the time that my grandfather was born in 1898, the British had been in charge for over a hundred years. No wonder then that come the turn of the century, Portuguese had long since been dropped as the family language and English was spoken instead. The British eventually converted the main church in Cochin to the Anglican communion, though they left the Catholic church on Vypeen untouched.

So there you have it. That's how come my mother's side of the family were English-speaking Catholics, born in India, of Portuguese descent. I'll get to my father's family later.

The most noticeable result for me today is that when I have to fill in any official forms that ask for ethnic identity, I invariably tick the box that says 'Other'.

One of the dishes I ate as a child in London comes straight from those early days of the Portuguese in India. It is vindaloo.

Vindaloo, which to me and my family has always been pronounced vin-*dah*-loo, is nothing at all like the vindaloos you get in standard British curry houses. The curry-house vindaloo seems to be primarily about heat. Indeed, the heat in a typical vindaloo is the whole point because it's so hot that you can't really taste anything else. So it's not so much a curry as a badge of laddishness. The vindaloo that I grew up with, while certainly hot, had a whole lot more going for it than just that. And for some reason we always ate it at Christmas.

Read the relevant books and authentic vindaloos are always claimed as being the invention of the Portuguese-Indian colony of Goa. But I, with absolutely no evidence to back this assertion up, would like to resolutely state that vindaloo was first created slightly further south in Cochin, Kerala. After all, Cochin was where the Portuguese first settled in India, so why shouldn't the people there have been the first ones to combine *vinho* (Portuguese for wine – but here meaning wine vinegar) with *alhos* (meaning garlic)?

Aside from adding a glorious sharpness of taste to a vindaloo, the vinegar used in it also acts as a preservative. Maybe that's why vindaloos are traditionally a dish served at celebrations. They can be cooked in advance and kept for several days. The vinegar, in effect, pickles the pork – the usual meat from which a vindaloo is made. Duck vindaloo is also popular, as ducks are plentiful in the flooded rice fields of southern India. Adapting a pork recipe to duck (and sometimes even chicken) made the dish accessible to both Muslims and Hindus.

In my memory vindaloo is made with fat chunks of pork, sometimes with beef added, and the occasional cooked beetroot also in the pan for some extra colour. (Though the beetroot was a secret addition of my grandmother's that she never willingly revealed to her daughters and which they only uncovered relatively late in the day.)

Vindaloo would be eaten for lunch on Christmas Day, but it would also, and more deliciously, have been eaten in the early hours of morning after a trip to midnight mass, scooped out of the large pans with hunks of fresh, white, crusty bread.

Even just writing about it I am straight back to my childhood, with a nest of hair that would make a haystack look well groomed, and outrageously flared brushed cotton loons in a fetching shade of orange, sleep tugging at my eyelids because here we are, in my grandmother's kitchen, eating curry at half one in the morning on Christmas Day. And yes, there may well have been a tank-top involved, because it was the 1970s and the world was a different place to what it is today. Then, after eating our fill, we would leave my grandmother's house, walk tiredly out into the cold night air and traipse round the corner to my uncle's house, where we would sleep for what was left of the night.

But I'm leaping ahead hundreds of years. What little I know about Francisco Rebello is based on a family tree compiled by a descendant of Antonio Fernandez – the other survivor of the shipwreck. The family tree mentions the shipwreck, the two survivors, intertwines the Fernandez family with the Rebello family, and leads all the way down to my mother.

Try to fathom out the intricacies of the family tree and in no time at all you're lost in a maze of second and third cousins with Portuguese names aplenty. There are Rosarios, Gomezs, Noranhos, Santos, Cardozas and Correas heading off in all directions. Somewhere near the start of the tree there is an ancestor recorded only as 'Manuvaal – Dutch Sailor Boy'. From what I can figure out he was the grandfather of my great grandfather. But stare at the names too long and the whole thing becomes a meaningless blur. And the records are far from complete.

Paper rotted easily in those tropical climes. And the churches were prone to the occasional round of pillage, as one religious group held temporary sway over another and papers were burned as a show of disdain. My mother has another theory as to why many branches on the tree have missing names. She thinks that the Portuguese community on the island of Vypeen, in years gone by, held typical colonial feelings of superiority over the indigenous population. So if someone from the community married someone from outside it, especially anyone from the interior of the island, perhaps the records were discreetly not kept.

Further down the family tree, British names start cropping up. How British the British names actually were is open to interpretation. One reason is that when British clergy arrived in India and started trying to recruit the locals to Christianity, they would often conduct mass conversions and, more importantly, mass baptisms. At these baptisms it was often the custom for the presiding clergyman to give the converts the same baptismal surname. And the surname they chose to confer on the new converts was often the clergyman's very own Christian name. So in many parts of India you can find local churchgoers whose surnames are Christian names.

Then you get cases of people like my grandmother. She married into the Rebello family tree in 1928. By then she was nineteen and had been born as Edith da Costa. However, she had three brothers. Three brothers who had their hearts set on being engineers. The biggest and best engineering firm to work for at the time was the British company Bruntons. But her parents knew that if the da Costa boys applied for apprenticeships under their family names they wouldn't even get an interview, let alone be taken on. So the family changed its name to Roberts. And it worked. The brothers got interviews. Which led to the apprenticeships and trades that were to stand them in such good stead throughout their lives.

My actual lineage on the family tree goes like this: Francisco Rebello was the father of Frederick, who was the father of Stephen, who was the father of Matthew (and eleven others), and Matthew was my grandfather. So that makes me only five generations on from a shipwrecked Portuguese sailor.

On my grandmother's side of things, I only have stories going back to the days of her parents. In the early 1900s her father was an engineer who was employed building the Great Indian Peninsular Railway. Life was rough and frugal. Families were constantly on the move. They had to clear jungles, drain swamps and make cuttings through hillsides. Everywhere they went they'd be up against not only the terrain, but mosquitoes, flies, rats, snakes, monsoon rains, scorching sun, occasional riots and typhoid, cholera and dysentery. And my grandmother remembered marksmen standing guard over the crews as they worked, keeping at bay the hyenas and cheetahs who would, from time to time, kill, drag off and eat a labourer.

But everywhere they went, new, glistening, steel-blue tracks proudly proclaimed the coming century and the seemingly endless domination of the British. Today, of course, the British, at least as lords and masters, have long since gone. But the tracks are still there. And still doing the job they were built for by, among many other people, my great-grandfather almost a hundred years ago.

Educated at various railway primary schools on her parents' travels through India, my grandmother had a further four years' secondary schooling at the Convent of Jesus and Mary, Poona, before returning to Vypeen in 1927 to care for her mother, who had fallen ill.

In 1928 she married my grandfather, Matthew Rebello, who was an accountant. In the same year they sailed for Rangoon in Burma, where my grandfather started to work for the British administration.

four

POTATO CURRY

These days, for me here in London, the only people I get coming to the door trying to sell things are those wanting to know if I'm happy with my gas supplier, or kids with plastic boxes of rubber gloves and fake chamois leathers, or Jehovah's Witnesses.

When my mother was growing up in Burma you'd get a whole different calibre of roadside-patter merchants hawking their wares. She lived in a flat in a building next to a mosque and all day long the street would be a roofless theatre throbbing with energy, the air alive with the cries of the vendors as they sought to catch your ear and, more deliciously, your nostrils.

Every morning she and her younger brothers and sisters would be awakened by cries in different languages – some lyrical, some strident, some wheedling – each designed to part you from what little cash you might have hidden away in your pockets. Few of the hawkers could afford to pay shop rents so they carried their goods on their heads or dangling from shoulder poles, or in overloaded backpacks, or balanced on small handcarts, all the while announcing and extolling their wares in bursts of song as instantly recognisable and as catchy as a Vitalite jingle.

To grab attention they would use bells, gongs, drums and clappers. Faces would be contorted into theatrical expressions. And above all else a tongue coated with honey would sweet-talk the listener. To succeed you needed not only to be seen, but to be heard. And not only heard, but heeded.

One of my mother's favourites was an Indian street-seller who crooned seductively as if lullabying a drowsy child to sleep:

> *Arg-ghee-ah,*
> *Arg-ghee-ah,*
> *Halva-wallah!*
>
> *I've come,*
> *I've come,*
> *The sweetmeat fellow!*

Some hawkers carried glowing embers in portable clay ovens to keep the food warm, low stools so that they could encourage customers to sit on the pavements anywhere along their route, and water for washing up their chopsticks, bowls and coconut shell spoons. Barbers and dentists also worked the streets, carrying out their trade alongside the traffic, as did the fortune-tellers and the vendors of charms, love potions and herbal remedies that invariably comprised villainous-looking, vile-smelling, shrivelled-up objects whose provenance one was never wise to enquire into too deeply.

The early morning callers acted as an alarm clock for my mother. Sometimes she was allocated a little money to buy what she fancied for breakfast. First she would consult her stomach to decide what it felt like eating. Would it be sweet? Or sour? Or chilli hot? Then she would listen intently. Then, when the cry of the seller who was serenading the delicacy of choice was heard, she would leap out of bed and rush to the window yelling for the seller to stop, 'Ooper-aow, jhuldi-jhuldi!' – 'Come upstairs, quick-quick!' Or she would run down with her own little bowl to be filled with the steaming or spicy or sweet-hot fancies.

Years later, when my mother became a storyteller in the primary schools of inner London, all the attention-grabbing techniques she had absorbed from the street-sellers as a child came back to her. And the listening skills she learned way back then also came into their own. For storytellers need not only supreme command of their material, but also an ear fine-tuned to the audience they are entertaining.

My mother's favourite among all the foods the wandering street-sellers would offer, and, indeed, my favourite when she prepared it for the family thirty years later and half a world away in South London, was a Burmese speciality called Ohn-No Kyaukswe. It is, in prosaic terms, a spicy chicken and coconut noodle soup. In more accurate terms it is, in my opinion, a bowl full of heaven.

This is my mother's recipe for it. In sharing it with you I am lending you the very finest jewel in my family's culinary crown. Please accord it the reverence it deserves. And don't share the recipe with anyone else. Just share the dish, and let them be blown away by your artistry. Incidentally, the quantity my mother gives in this recipe produces enough kyaukswe to serve ten people. It's that kind of dish. (Mind you, having said that, whenever I've cooked it using my mother's measures, I've never needed ten people to polish it off. I mean, it might take a couple of days, but we get there. Or, as my wife so accurately says, 'When it comes to kyaukswe, there is no off switch.')

CHICKEN KYAUKSWE
SERVES 10

oil for frying
9 medium onions, grated
6 large cloves garlic, crushed
fresh ginger (2 Oxo-cube-size), pounded
3½ teaspoons turmeric
4 teaspoons chilli powder
5lb chicken thighs
4 chicken breasts, chopped in bite-size pieces
1½ blocks (300g) coconut cream
4 teaspoons salt
16 tablespoons lemon juice
18 tablespoons gram flour

Put oil in the bottom of a large pan. Add the onions, garlic and ginger and fry a little. Add the turmeric and chilli powder, and cook some more making sure the spices don't burn. Add the chicken and fry a little. Add the coconut cream, a good deal of the salt and lemon juice, and 4½ pints of water. Mix the gram flour into a smooth paste with a little water and add this, 4 spoons at a time, into the pan to thicken the gravy, stirring as you do so. Cook over gentle heat for 30–40 minutes, tasting as it cooks, and adding salt, lemon and flour paste as necessary.

Serve over egg noodles, accompanied with little bowls of crushed roasted chilli, chopped-up spring onions, hard-boiled eggs cut into quarters and lemon wedges.

And this is how you eat it.

Put a portion of noodles into a deep bowl. Then ladle over the kyaukswe gravy along with a few pieces of chicken. (Or 'drown it in the gravy', as kyaukswe novices were always instructed at our family table.) Then let each diner add as few, or as many, of the accompanying garnishes as they wish to create the precise combinations of flavour that will most seduce their palate. Then eat with abandon. And slurping is most definitely allowed.

One last thing. Don't wear a white shirt.

My grandfather went to Burma because there were jobs there. It was one of those typically British colonial arrangements. People from one part of the empire were relocated to another part in order to administer the affairs of the people who lived there. That way the people like my grandfather who were helping the British run things owed more allegiance to the empire than they did to the local populace.

The British had been in Burma since 1824. First they captured the parts of Burma to the east of the Indian border in order to 'protect' that border. Then, in 1852, in the second Anglo-Burmese war, they seized the rest of lower Burma. (The fact that there had even been one Anglo-Burmese war was news to me.) Then, in 1885, in the third war, Mandalay was captured and hence the whole country came under British rule. Less than a year after that, Burma was designated a province of India and, as such, became a colony of the empire.

Over fifty years later Bing Crosby and Bob Hope made a movie about the road to Mandalay. However, in terms of giving you an insight into the prevailing political, social and cultural conditions of Burma, it isn't really much use. The jokes, however, are funny. Sort of.

My grandfather worked as an accountant for the Indian government, which was now, under British Empire logic, running Burma. And it seems he bought the whole deal. He believed in Britain, British values and the British Empire. Mind you, as he worked for the British Empire, he was on the inside of the system and one of the – relatively – favoured few. He knew by heart the poetry of Milton and Wordsworth. He was always impeccably turned out in a suit and a tie. And, undoubtedly, if he didn't quite view Britain as the Mother Country, he believed that it was at least a fine and fair Stepmother Country. (Only later was he to discover that stepmothers aren't always overjoyed when their adoptive children turn up.)

Life in Rangoon was good to my grandparents. My grandfather went to work every day and added up rows of figures that showed just how well the colony was being run. Burma was a rich and prosperous land. Thanks to its productive paddy fields, it was called the 'rice bowl of Asia'. Minerals and precious stones were also to be found in abundance. And its teak forests and rubber plantations became famous the world over.

My grandmother set up home in a spacious flat on 42nd Street. And while her husband built a career in the civil administration, she set about creating the family of which she had always dreamt. In 1929 a son was born. Then, a year later, a daughter. The son, who would be looked up to and respected and loved by all his siblings, would be the one who would pioneer the family's move to England. The daughter would become my mother.

Though the family were far from wealthy, as this was the east a servant – the ayah – was employed to help run the household. She cooked and cleaned and looked after the children and did much else besides. The ayah's son, accorded the status of chokra, would also help out with small jobs like polishing shoes and delivering by bike freshly cooked tiffin carriers of food for the children at school lunchtimes. Sometimes the ayah's husband would also appear to help out with heavy, manual jobs like fixing doors or shifting furniture.

To my ears 'servant' is a loaded word. I suppose it is tainted by the legacy of the colonial 'master and servant' relationship. However, the way things worked in my grandparents' household, the word 'servant' never had any connotation of inferiority. The people who worked for the family were viewed as an au pair might be today, or someone who comes in once a week to clean your house – except the ayah's was a more trusted, and valued, position. They stayed with the family for a long time. And though undoubtedly a hierarchy did exist, they were a respected and often loved part of the family.

One of the main implications of being able to hire help was that all the time my grandmother lived in Burma she didn't do much cooking. Yes, she would specify what was to be bought on the ayah's early morning trips to the market where the freshest of produce, the finest meat or fish straight from the sea was always eagerly haggled over, and back at home she would discuss what was to be cooked that particular day, but the actual cooking was primarily left to the ayah to do.

During the rest of the day my grandmother had her hands full organising the family and looking after the children. Though her hands may well have been full, my mother remembers them as always being immaculately manicured with the French polish that was the height of fashion over in Europe.

Their social life centred around the local Catholic church, or in entertaining friends at home, all of whom had some kind of Indo-Portuguese links. Food would always be key in these gatherings. As with immigrants the world over, food from the old country would get people talking and laughing, and reminiscing about earlier times.

For my mother, born during the monsoon season in 1930, it was an idyllic world in which to grow up. It was safe, it was friendly, and an order existed which meant she could get on with the all-consuming business of being a child. Favourite among her toys were an old wooden rocking horse with one ear missing, a small collection of well-worn teddy bears and a doll's house whose capacious insides surprisingly housed only four people.

In a cage on the kitchen table lived Rupert, a pet Java sparrow, who would sweetly serenade the household every morning and had somewhat poignantly been named after the hero of *The Prisoner of Zenda*. Larger pets were out of the question as the family home was a flat two flights of stairs up from a coffee shop. However, all this changed when an uncle, who worked as an engineer on the ships, stopped by en route to Australia and knocked on the door with a large turkey under his arm. The turkey, all haughty demeanour and proprietary head swivels, ended up tied to the leg of the kitchen table. Every afternoon when she got back from school, my mum, accompanied by the other children, would take the turkey out for a walk. Getting a reluctant turkey on a string lead down two flights of stairs is no mean feat. Once down at ground level, the main road would have to be crossed, and so my mum's elder brother would solemnly hold his hand up to stop the traffic. The turkey remained dignified and noble throughout.

Christmas, that year, was a great success.

My mother went to school at the Branch Convent in Judah Ezekial Street and was taught by nuns of the Good Shepherd order. The school was two streets away from St Mary's Cathedral – the heart of the Rangoon Catholic community. The standards of education were high and the discipline was as crisp as the white cotton shirts the girls had to wear. God, of course, lurked around every corner of the school day. And if they didn't get enough God at school, or at Sunday mass, or by going to confession, there were also the occasional retreats run by a group of Irish missionaries called the Redemptorists. My mother remembers sitting terrified in a pew, hands clasped tightly together on her lap, as the conviction-laden voices of the Redemptorists rained down hellfire and damnation and guilt upon the congregation of supposed sinners.

The streets, dry and dusty in summer, awash with small rivers in the rainy season, doubled as playgrounds. Rollerskates, skipping ropes, bikes and scooters all took a fair battering. Carved wooden tops, spun with string, danced on paving stones. And circles of children would form to play chi-loong with a woven rattan ball that had to be kept up using feet, heads, knees, elbows and shoulders, but never hands.

When the winds came kites were made at home on the kitchen table or bought from the kite-makers in fantastic shapes of dragons or fishes or butterflies. Then the limpid blue sky would come alive with colours as bright as the rolls of cotton on the night market stalls. My mother's brothers, all expert fliers, would glue ground glass to the strings of their kites, then carry them out to the open spaces to scramble them into action whenever an enemy kite wheeled into view. The trick was to fly your kite so that the ground-glass-covered string intersected the string of your rival's, rubbing against it, cutting the line and leaving the victim to flutter, lifeless, to the ground or into the welcoming branches of a nearby tree. Then all the children who had gathered to watch the aerial dogfight would sprint off towards the downed dragon, fish or butterfly, each shouting out the universal, incontrovertible childhood law of 'finders keepers'.

Of course, the mad tropicality of the encroaching forests was never far away. As a place to play it was an environment that held too many potential dangers to be a truly carefree Eden. My mother was constantly reminded that even the most innocuous-looking patch of grass could easily conceal one of Burma's 'fifty-two venomous snakes'. And whenever she went to put on her shoes, she would first assiduously tip each one up in turn to flush out any scorpion that might be lurking there, attracted by the warmth and the dark.

But what my mother remembers, and misses, most about the world she grew up in was the camaraderie. Everyone got on with everyone else, each helped out the other when they were in need, and when you played in the streets you were just as likely to be trying to win marbles from a fellow grinning urchin who was Buddhist or Muslim, Sikh or Hindu. The only obvious absentees from the United Nations of the playground were the British. The British kept themselves resolutely to themselves. They only really cared about the running of their empire and the cucumber-sandwiched gossip of Rangoon's three great clubs: the Pegu, the Boat and the Gymkhana. Clubs that were strictly for whites only.

Had the British only ventured out among the 'natives' with a more open mind they would have found a world in which a myriad of cultures had forged a way to live and work together on a basis of shared respect. And, as my mum most gloriously attests, shared food. Wander into the home of any of her Burmese friends and she would be welcomed by the standard greeting, not of 'Hello' or 'How are you?' or 'Come in', but by the phrase, 'Htamin sa pee bee la?' – 'Have you eaten yet?' And whether she had or hadn't eaten already she always found room for a little more. Come the eve of the Muslim festival of Eid, the landlord of the family's flat, who also owned the coffee shop on the ground floor, would hire cooks to chop, fry and stir through the night, preparing vast mountains of lamb biriani that would be served to all his tenants the following day. Indeed, every festival of every religion, was carefully filed in my mum's mind, cross-referenced with which house she and her siblings should make a beeline for in order to scoff the best food. The food in question was always dished up freely, and indeed joyfully, as everyone shared the hospitable belief that to welcome another to your table was to bring down a blessing on your home. Even when my mother was older and had a temporary job collecting the census, she would find herself invited to share the food of the poorest homes she visited, despite the fact that it would often be that family's only meal of the day. But as I said, it was a society where everyone looked out for each other, and as she left she would always discreetly leave a little money tucked under her bowl.

The build-up to Christmas in 1941 was, to say the least, odd. The family had by now grown to eight people so the once spacious flat was somewhat cramped. But Christmas, as ever, was a time for the children, so the crowded rooms buzzed with quietly growing excitement. Despite the encroaching war the family did all the things they usually did. Elaborate menus were discussed and debated. Food was ordered and stocked well in advance. New clothes for the big day were commissioned from the tailors. And the expectant children tried to imagine what presents they might get come Christmas morning.

All the while the Japanese were moving in on the country. Fearing that Rangoon was no longer safe, my grandparents shut up the flat on 42nd Street and moved the family out of town to a nearby village. My mother, who would have been eleven, remembers locking up her toys in a tall wooden cupboard and writing a note that she stuck to the door:

Nobody touch my things.
I shall return.
  Z

She had just seen the movie *The Mask of Zorro* and so was convinced that a slashed 'Z' would scare potential thieves away.

The first bombs fell on Rangoon on the twenty-third of December, 1941.

I once found, hidden away in the cellar of the South London house I grew up in, a small, battered tin suitcase that dates back to those days. Inside it, wrapped in yellowed and disintegrating newspaper, I uncovered three chunks of twisted black metal. I took the metal out of the cellar and asked my mother what these treasured relics were. She looked at them for a while, struggling to remember things she'd probably rather forget, then said that they were pieces of shrapnel her brother had collected from the jungle near where they were staying the day after the first Japanese bombing raid. I re-wrapped them in the remnants of the newspaper and put them back in the tin suitcase. It struck me as a very odd thing to hang on to. But, in retrospect, it was these bombs, and the threat of more of them, that completely changed the way my family saw the world around them.

As the Japanese advanced there seemed to be no one to stop them. The British, so long seen as the greatest power in the world, were shown to be unready and unequipped. And there was an undoubted seismic shock throughout the east when it woke up to the fact that the white man, so long the master, was no longer invincible. Under the onslaught of the Japanese advance not only was resistance being defeated and territory claimed, but an old order was also crumbling.

But in places it crumbled slowly. For even as the Japanese rampaged on, my mother remembers that her father and many others held on to a touching but misguided belief that British planes would soon take to the skies and turn the invaders back. Little did they know that there were hardly any British planes around, and what planes could be found were both old and ill-equipped. And anyway, the harsh truth was that for the British Empire as a whole there were more pressing problems in a Europe over-run by Hitler's Third Reich. So the difficulties facing Burma were way down the list of priorities.

The day after that first bombing raid, my mother and the other children caught a bus to go into town and pick up the new shoes that had been made for them by the Chinese shoemaker. As the bus stopped and the children excitedly got off, the wail of an air-raid siren ripped through the air. Unsure what to do, they turned to their mother who hurried them towards the shoemaker's shop. They were barely all inside the door when the first explosion started to shake the building. Excitement turned to fear. The next bomb fell closer to the shop and blew in some of its windows. Trying to escape the threat of further flying glass, the Chinese shoemaker urgently pressed all the family into the only room in the building that didn't have windows – the toilet. My mother remembers cramming round the edges of the toilet – which was essentially a hole in the floor for squatting over – with the rest of the family, silently pray-ing as the bombs fell closer and closer. After the last explosion had sounded, my grandmother kept them in place for an age just in case the planes came back. Eventually they ventured out into the chaos of the shoe-maker's shop. My grandmother thanked the shoemaker for his 'hospitality', paid for the shoes that, somehow, had remained unscathed and took the children back to the village on the next bus. As the road was pockmarked with bomb craters the journey home took twice as long as the journey out. And children, being children, counted the dead bodies they saw all the way home. By the time they got back to the village house, they had all been on a journey far longer than one that you could just measure in miles.

It's hard to say when, precisely, anyone grows up. When, exactly, do you stop seeing the world through a child's eyes? When do you realise that there is as much, if not more, rain in the world than sunshine? More tears than laughter. And maybe more to fill you with fear than to fill you with hope. I think, perhaps, on that long ride home, that my mother grew up.

Or maybe it was a few days later. On a trip to a nearby market.

Markets in the east are a thing of wonder. In a space that was empty and barren just a few hours before, life erupts like flowers in a desert after a flash flood has watered it. Traders set up temporary shop – territories carefully defined – and arrange their goods to catch the eye of the customers who will soon be wandering the newly created alleyways in search of bargains. Some arrange their displays with all the skill of the finest department-store window dressers. Some rely on the sheer quality of their fruit and vegetables to make the sale and just pile it high and let the enticing and intriguing shapes and colours do all the hard work. And some, hawking food cooked on the spot over small wood-burning stoves, know that the sizzle of oil, the siren call of aroma and the occasional small sample handed out with a smile will soon have customers buzzing about like moths round a hurricane lamp.

In Burma there were two kinds of market. First there was the morning market where you would go primarily to buy fresh produce. With stalls set up as the sun crept from behind the horizon, you would find meat freshly slaughtered, plump and scrawny chickens clucking under baskets, crabs in wet boxes slowly clambering sideways over each other as if jostling for a slightly better vantage point, and all manner of fish twitching and glistening and gulping air. Then there were the stalls selling vegetables. And the stalls selling fruit. Fruit like mangoes, papaws, durians, jackfruit, breadfruit, mangosteens, rambutans, maryans, coconuts, guavas, star fruit and the Burmese plums zen-dees, and much else besides. The morning markets were where people would come for the food shopping that would feed their families for the day ahead. Shopping, especially for things like meat and fish, was a daily affair as few people had fridges to keep food fresh. So you bought what you needed each morning from the market. By midday, as the sun had climbed to its imperious zenith, the heat would be so intense that the morning market would be all but closed. The stallholders and traders would be heading home, counting their takings and looking forward to something to eat after their long morning's labour.

The other type of market was the night market. And while the morning market was all about the daily practicalities of shopping for what you needed, the night market always had a slight feel of the fairground bazaar about it.

Maybe it was the darkness that lapped at its edges, or the glow of the hurricane lamps, or the very fact that it was at the end of the working day and the heat in the air was softer and more caressing. So the inclination of the crowds was to meander through the stalls. The urgency of the morning market was gone, and an amiable languor replaced it. The night market was where you would go to buy dry goods. You'd find cheap clothes, bales of cotton and silk, sandals and shoes, pots, pans and all kinds of hardware, and stalls selling trinkets and toys laid out to entice and delight the small eyes of children as they darted away from their parents and weaved their own paths through the ambling forest of grown-ups' legs. Today, in the west, people stroll through a mall just to see what's around. In the east, and especially the east of sixty years ago, the night market functioned as just the same kind of social space. Even if you didn't end up buying much, or indeed anything at all, a circuit of the night market was for many a much-loved part of the daily routine.

Three days after Christmas 1941, my mother went to the morning market she always loved to visit when she didn't have school. By then many of the stallholders and traders knew her and knew that she came from a large family who all had to be fed. As she walked past they would smile and joke and try to convince her of the irresistibility of their goods. But she would invariably be heading for the mat set up by the Indian sweet-seller. He would pile up glistening sugar-sweet pyramids of gulab jams, ladhus, jellabies and all manner of boiled-milk delicacies, and sit behind them, bare-bellied and saronged, serenading the passers-by with entreaties to indulge.

The problem with the air-raid sirens was that, despite the attack a few days earlier, no one took them too seriously. In the weeks up to Christmas their wails had rent the air on many occasions. But raids had never come. People who at first had run for cover got blasé about it all. They just cocked their heads to one side, checked what everyone else was doing, then assigned the sound of the horns the status of just another addition to the city's cacophonous chorus.

The problem with markets is that they are soft targets. There are no buildings to shelter in. And there are lots of people to kill.

By the time my mother got to the market, the Japanese planes had long wheeled away towards the sun. But in their wake they had left a bloody calling card. Stalls were over-turned. Chickens ran free. Sacks of bullet-riddled rice spilled their guts onto the dusty earth. And there were bodies everywhere.

When she eventually reached the Indian sweet-seller, things didn't look too bad. The sweets still stood proudly in their glistening pyramids. And the sweet-seller still sat bare-bellied behind them. Only his head was tipped forward with his chin resting on his chest. And his eyes were closed. It looked like he was asleep. But he wasn't breathing. He wasn't breathing at all. And seeping out from under where he sat was a slowly advancing tide of darkness.

Perhaps that's when my mother grew up.

* * *

In the weeks that followed things started to fall apart. The raids became more frequent. Civil order frayed and cracked. People started to think about escape. Those with no real tie to the country, like the Indian labourers, packed up what little they had and began the long walk back to their homeland.

In my mother's home, when the children were asleep, talk circled round and round and spiralled down onto the need to get the family out. By then my grandfather, who was at heart a gentle soul, was daily having to face the reality of their predicament. Long an accountant for the administration, the mounting chaos all around had led him to be seconded to a different department. His job had changed out of all recognition. Yes, he was still adding up, but now instead of counting money, or government workers, or bags of cement needed to build a new bridge, he was counting dead bodies. After every air raid he would climb into a small flat-backed truck and drive along the path that the bombers had taken. As he went he would count and pinpoint the corpses. Then he would return to his office and hand over the paperwork so that if a crew of labourers could be found, they could go out and collect the bodies. At first they always tried to accord each deceased the dignity of an individual grave. But soon there were just too many bodies, and practicality, coupled with the fear of disease, meant that many of those killed found their final resting place somewhat crowded.

In one crucial respect, however, my grandfather was a very lucky man. That's because he worked for the government. And though he wasn't that important in the grand scheme of things, the government did make some effort to look after its own. On the first of February 1942, a whispered message was passed to him. The last boat out of Rangoon was leaving the next morning. There was no time to issue tickets. There was just a location. Get your family, get a small bag of what you could carry, get down to the river and get on that boat. And don't tell anyone else.

My grandparents, to their credit, let their friends know what was going on. After all, these were people they cared about and loved, so how could they not share with them information that may well save their lives? And when order is breaking down all around you, if you can't count on your friends, then who can you count on?

That night my grandmother hurriedly packed bags for her family. The next morning she woke the children early and helped them dress as they rubbed sleep from their eyes. Then the whole family, including her mother who had been living with them for years, headed off to the river. By the time they reached the appointed spot it was clear that word had spread. The bank of the Irrawaddy River where the SS *Chilka* was moored was awash with people.

With great difficulty my grandparents forced a way through the crowd. By the time they reached the foot of the gangplank, what had been a melee had turned into a near riot. My mother remembers looking up at that plank of wood that climbed towards the boat at a forty-five-degree angle and wobbled and shuddered under the weight of people pushing and shoving their way up. Her mother, clutching her baby son to her chest, gathered her family round her and issued shouted instructions above the mael-strom that enveloped them. In the critical minutes that lay ahead they were bound to get separated. If that happened, no one was to panic. Each older child was to hold onto the hand of a younger child and never let go. And, come what may, they were going to get on the boat. They were all going to get on the boat.

Then the air-raid sirens sounded. The crowds, for an instant, fell silent. And the chainsaw buzz of aeroplane engines filled the air.

There had been no order before, but now panic started grabbing at people. Those near the bottom of the gang-plank started fighting to get on. But then people already on the boat, fearing that they had only succeeded in getting aboard a sitting duck, turned round and tried to force their way back down the narrow piece of wood they had just strived so hard to climb up. The old lady, my mum's grand-mother, viewed the situation and decided that her duty lay in giving up her place so that her grandchildren could escape. She refused to budge from the shore and with beads in hand started frantically reciting the rosary and imploring the others to leave her behind. 'Our Lady, the Blessed Virgin Mary, help us in our troubles ... don't worry about me ... you are young, you go on ... I'm old, don't let me be a burden ... save yourselves, God will look after me.'

In the chaos that followed, as the planes mosquitoed in on the SS *Chilka*, my mother remembers watching as people jumped or just fell from the gangplank and were washed downstream in the fast-flowing waters of the Irrawaddy. And she remembers the whole family being corralled behind her grandmother, her still praying and protesting grandmother, to form a scrum to force her up the gangplank. Somehow, in the mayhem, everybody made it on board.

The planes, two of them, most likely Zero fighter-bombers, made their first pass over the boat sizing up the hapless prey. Then they flew off towards the rising sun and everyone aboard the *Chilka* stood still and watched them. The planes wheeled back, arcing upwards to gain altitude from which to dive down towards the boat. All hell broke loose. People desperately sought out whatever cover could be found. As the planes droned in, the air was filled with screaming and crying and softly muttered prayers.

Even with her eyes closed my mother could hear the sound of the engines getting closer and closer and closer. And then the sound of the engines started to recede. My mother opened her eyes and watched as the Japanese planes flew on and on away from the boat. Without firing a single shot.

On the second of February 1942 the SS *Chilka* left the chaos of Rangoon for the safety of Calcutta.

As the boat set sail it was crammed with far more people than it could safely carry. But the captain, knowing that this was the last boat out of Rangoon before it would fall to the Japanese, was determined to get as many people away as he could.

There were nine in my grandparents' party and they had to sleep wherever there was space. More by luck than by design, they discovered a tiny cabin, the size of a large cupboard, where the old lady could sleep. My aunt, then just six years old, was ill at the time, so she too stayed in the cabin. My mother remembers bedding down under a table somewhere. And she remembers her father having to barter possessions to get food from whomever he could on the boat. But what food there was soon ran out. The first problem was the sheer number of people aboard. The second was that in order to dodge Japanese submarines, instead of taking a direct route to Calcutta straight across the Bay of Bengal, the captain of the SS *Chilka* opted to hug the coastline, thus making the journey last far longer than usual.

For the last two days there was no food to be had anywhere. Having seen how my own children get after missing just a single meal, it's hard to imagine how my grandparents handled six children who had no food for two days. But I suppose the truth is that these were very different days. And everyone was just glad to be alive on a boat that, hour by hour, was taking them closer and closer to safety.

In Calcutta the people knew that the boat had left Rangoon, but after that there had been no word. That's because the captain, fearing interception of his signals, had not radioed his plan to hug the coast to avoid the submarines. Soon the boat was a day overdue. And then another day. And then another day. The waiting families and friends of those aboard the SS *Chilka* knew that the worst had happened. The boat had been sunk. And, probably, everyone lost.

When word first got out that the *Chilka* had been spotted up the coast from Calcutta, it was a miracle. The news spread like wildfire among the same people who had just begun to mourn the loss of their loved ones. Even those who had no connection with anyone on the boat took its seeming return from the dead as a beacon of hope in a world that was growing darker by the day.

As the SS *Chilka* edged slowly towards the docks in Calcutta, my mother could not believe the welcome that awaited them. A flotilla of small boats escorted them in. On the quayside brightly coloured bunting fluttered in the sun, bands blasted out joyful music, and people were everywhere shouting and cheering and thanking whatever god or gods they believed in. My mother remembers peering out of a porthole with her brothers and sisters wedged against her as people on the quayside threw oranges up for them to catch.

They had escaped. They had survived.

And they had been lucky because they had caught a boat out of Burma. Other friends were not so fortunate. I have in my possession a photocopy of a handwritten account of how the Morais family, people my mother had grown up with, had got out of the country. First they had crammed into cattle trucks on a train, '255 people per van'. But the tracks had been bombed and the train was derailed, killing at least twenty and injuring many more. Then they cadged lifts upriver on launches. Then they had to walk, for mile after mile, along jungle tracks made muddy by torrential rains. Much of the way was up steep, overgrown hillsides. Each step was often a battle against the terrain, the weather and physical exhaustion. At one point they reached a camp just as the grandmother of the party collapsed and could walk no further. The next morning they approached the British camp commandant to see if space could be found on the train of elephants that was leaving that day. The response was far from sympathetic:

'Lady, I am to sacrifice my kit for your mother?'

The kit in question was a radio, clothing and camp furniture. The account goes on, with great restraint: 'No sacrifice was ever demanded, for room there was plenty on the three elephants going out – but evidently the jungle life had made him forget the existence of a war.'

Eventually they too made it out of Burma, largely on foot, and into the safety of Calcutta. And en route, while many just passed by on the other side too preoccupied with their own survival, they were also helped by people they didn't know, and other British soldiers and Burmese guides. So maybe it's true that war brings out the worst, and the best, in people. Their highest praise goes to another group of travellers.

In our absence some Gurkha evacuees seeing the sad plight of my parents carried my father for a mile near the stream where they were camping, and moreover with food, water and other means revived the old man. No words could ever thank them for their kindness in our hour of need, but perhaps by my deeds I may one day repay them.

So, all things considered, my mother's family were lucky. It could all have been so much worse, so very easily.

The SS *Chilka*, after unloading in Calcutta the people it had rescued from Rangoon, refuelled, restocked and turned round to head back to Burma to try one more rescue mission. But its luck had run out. Before it reached Rangoon it was sunk by Japanese torpedoes.

Over sixty years later I accompanied my mother on a trip to visit my aunt, who lived in Malacca in Malaysia. I asked her what she remembered of the boat out of Burma. Although it had been such a long time ago, and she had been ill on the boat and was only six years old at the time, certain memories were indelibly burned into her very being. She remembered being sick. She remembered sharing a cabin with her grandmother. And she remembered the boat's joyous reception when, finally, it arrived in Calcutta.

As the welcoming masses swarmed up the gangplank from the quayside, they carried tin buckets filled to the brim with food. Once they reached the hungry passengers they started handing out the food as fast as they could. The food was potato curry and freshly made chapattis. It was simple food. It was cheap food. But it was the first food that the people on the boat had eaten in days.

As my aunt spoke her eyes filled with tears and you could see that she could still taste that first mouthful of potato curry from over sixty years before. When the moment had passed and she was back in the present day, she turned to me and wistfully said that ever since then a simple potato curry had always been the best food she could eat.

And whenever she did eat it she knew she was eating something special. And she knew she was safe.

POTATO CURRY
SERVES 4

8 medium-sized potatoes
3 tablespoons oil
3 medium onions, sliced fine
1 teaspoon brown mustard seeds
6 curry leaves
1 teaspoon ginger paste
1 teaspoon garlic paste
1 teaspoon cumin powder
1 teaspoon coriander powder
1 tablespoon yogurt
1 teaspoon turmeric
½ teaspoon chilli powder
1 teaspoon salt
lemon juice, to taste

Cut the potatoes into 1-inch cubes and boil them until just cooked. Meanwhile, heat the oil and fry the onions until golden brown. Add the mustard seeds and curry leaves and fry briefly. Add ginger, garlic, cumin and coriander and fry for 1 minute. Add yogurt, turmeric and chilli, and cook over medium heat for 2–3 minutes.

Drain the potatoes, stir them in, then add half a cup of water. Simmer for 8–10 minutes. Add lemon juice and salt to taste.

five
THE LOOKERS-IN

I know less about my father's childhood than I do about my mother's. It's not that there is less to tell, it's just that the people who could tell the tales aren't really around any more. And he himself never talked about his childhood. I didn't think much about this when I was young. And it didn't occur to me to ask any questions. I was too caught up in my own life. On top of that, unlike my mother, my father had no relatives living in this country as I was growing up. His sister lived in the Netherlands. His brother had stayed in Ceylon. So whenever we had 'family' gatherings in London, they would essentially be for my mother's family. On the relatively rare occasions that my father's sister or brother came over to England, I don't think I ever heard them talk about their younger days. My father's life seemed to be 100 per cent based in London. This was his world. And the world he had once come from was more than just thousands of miles away.

When I was in my early teens, I went with my family on a trip to what had now become Sri Lanka. The first night we were there, staying at my uncle's house, some of my father's old friends came round and shared drinks with him late into the night. It was about the only time I ever saw him even slightly drunk. But that evening aside, nothing on the trip, or the travels we made while we were there, gave me the impression that my father had 'come home'. Maybe there was a slight tug of regret as we boarded the plane to fly back to England. But if it was there, it was not great. My father had made his choices almost forty years earlier. And if what little I have managed to learn about his early days is true, he made the right choices.

As I write, two pictures of my father are propped up on my desk. In the first he can't be more than eight or nine years old – a little older than my daughter is today – and he is dressed as a boy scout. He stands with twenty or so friends, stacked up in three rows, on the dusty earth of a tropical playing field, staring towards the camera with wide eyes, not knowing what lies ahead of him. The second picture was taken almost sixty years later at our family home in South London. A long table covered with a white table-cloth stretches away from the viewer. At the far end of the table, an eight-foot-high Christmas tree stands in the bay window. It is covered with silver baubles, white fairy lights and candles. The lights are on, but the candles aren't lit yet. The table is set for Christmas lunch, so the picture must have been taken on Christmas Eve. There are places for twenty people, with folded napkins on every plate, and garish gold and green crackers alongside. On the left of the picture is an old upright piano that no one ever played. On the walls of the room hang two of my father's paintings. And at the back of the room, between the Christmas tree and the piano, my father is asleep in a chair with his arms folded.

In the space between these two photographs there is a whole lifetime.

Christmas for me is always the 1970s. Today as I navigate one Christmas after another with my own children, I can't help but feel that it is a pale imitation of what Christmas is really all about. Of course, the excitement in the children's eyes as they get caught up in the blissful madness of it all is wonderful to see, but somehow it's just not the same. Perhaps it's similar for everyone. Perhaps everyone's idea of Christmas is stamped with whatever experiences they had as a child. When they, when we, all still believed. Before we realised that Father Christmas was actually our parents, that there wouldn't be peace on earth, and that presents are only things.

I was eight years old in 1970. And I was eighteen in 1980. I started the decade in short trousers, worrying about what part I'd get in the school nativity play, and with Noddy Holder incessantly screaming 'It's Christmas!' from every available transistor radio. I ended it just back from my first term at university, all big hair and charity shop chic, clutching a well-worn twelve-inch single of 'Blank Generation' by Richard Hell and the Voidoids. So I grew up in the 1970s. Or at least I grew older. Some things, however, never changed.

Christmas 1970 I came home from school at the end of term dreaming of getting a kiss from Brenda Kelly. Christmas 1980 I came home from university at the end of term hoping to get a snog from a girl I'll just call 'M'.

Let's just say that on both occasions, ten years apart, Mud's 'Lonely This Christmas' could well have been my theme song.

In the 1970s our house in South London was invariably the setting for Christmas celebrations, where our already extended family would open its arms even wider and sweep up whatever friends or distant relatives happened to be in town. There were two main reasons for this. First, my mother was the first of the brothers and sisters to get married and set up a home. The second reason is that we had the biggest house. It was a double-fronted Victorian villa in a then unfashionable and un-upcoming part of South London, which my parents were able to buy relatively cheaply and gradually do up as time and money became available.

The house had big rooms, high ceilings and loads of space for two growing kids and all their friends to play in during the holidays. It was furnished with bits and pieces my parents accumulated over the years. Much of the furniture was the heavy, out-of-favour Victorian antiques no one wanted any more. As there wasn't much demand, my mother could pick up much of what we needed to furnish the house without breaking the bank. But occasionally she would spot pieces she fell in love with that had to be bought whatever the cost.

There were once-regal sofas that now sagged in places like a bad facelift. There were imposing, mirrored wardrobes that still reeked of mothballs and in the back of which you fully expected to find a lion, a witch and a lamppost in the snow. And there was a beautiful, circular, mahogany dining table that Mick Carrol sat on and broke on the night of my eighteenth birthday party. (My father, to my eternal gratitude, took the disaster in his stride and, not wanting to ruin the party for me, just helped clear up the mess. He fixed the table the next day with blue nylon rope wrapped tightly round the central strut that had snapped. Twenty-five years on the table is still in the same dining room. And so is the rope.)

Come Christmas the main rooms of the house would be transformed. Strips of gummed coloured paper would be looped together in long lines and hung from the walls. Crinkled crepe streamers stored up all year would be carefully unrolled and Sellotaped to one corner of the ceiling before being twisted all the way across to the corner diagonally opposite.

Balloons would have to be lung-burstingly blown up as the cardboard-tube balloon pump would invariably have stopped working. Then me and my brother would spend ages vigorously rubbing the balloons up and down the sleeves of our gaudy jumpers, trying to generate enough static electricity to stick them to the walls. And it would work. For a few hours at least. Then we would return to the room to find that the balloons had slid, like an apologetic drunk, quietly to the floor. So we would gather them up and get out the Sellotape again. And Christmas cards would be displayed on every available flat surface.

Then, in the week before Christmas, my father would go and buy the tree. As the rooms in the house had high ceilings, my father would always struggle back from his expedition carrying a tree that was at least eight feet tall. It would take pride of place in the bay window in the double-length reception room that ran from the front to the back of the house. The task of getting the tree to stand up straight seemed to take as much time and effort as it later did to erect the London Eye. The bottom of the tree would be wedged into a bucket crammed with rolled-up balls of newspaper. Then it would be pushed this way and that until it was finally vertical. And then we would all move hurriedly away from it just in case it wasn't wedged in as tightly as it needed to be and it crashed down on our heads. The whole endeavour was a mixture of engineering, trial and error, and prayer. Invariably, God listened. And, frankly, he'd have been foolish not to. After all, we were doing it all for him. Well, for him and the presents.

After the tree was up we'd get the chance to decorate it. Boxes of cherished fragile ornaments would be retrieved from the attic. Layers of dust would be brushed aside as we opened the battered box lids. Reverentially, multicoloured globes would be removed and carefully hung on the tree. Long snakes of silver tinsel would be awoken from their hibernation in a plastic carrier bag, then they would be draped over the branches of the tree like feather boas round the shoulders of an excessively eye-shadowed partygoer dancing down the street with her high heels in her hand. Tin candleholders would be clipped to the tree and white candles – always white candles – angled into them so that as little melted wax as possible would drip onto the well-worn carpet below. Then fairy lights would be added. And when the tree was ready we'd turn out all the lights in the house and flick the switch while my father lit the candles.

Then we'd stand back, as a family, and admire our efforts.

On Christmas Eve the table would be set for lunch the next day. Except that it wouldn't be one table, but two or three arranged in a line. Each table would be a slightly different height to the one next to it. Which would be fine, unless you were unfortunate enough to end up with your plate on the tectonic fault line between two of them. Then things would get interesting. Especially as Brussels sprouts don't require much of an inclination to roll down a plate.

In the picture where my father is asleep, the table that seats twenty actually takes up only half the room. The other half of the room, behind where the photographer is standing, would contain two smaller tables. These would seat another ten or more people, usually the children. So Christmas lunch could easily end up with thirty or more people sitting down to eat.

Chairs were always a problem. After all, who has thirty chairs in a house? Not us, that's for sure. Every available seat, of every shape and size, was pressed into service. And my mother's voice could be heard the night before constantly on the phone, asking people to bring chairs. And cutlery. We never had enough cutlery. Chair-wise, however, the short straw was the high stool. Useful though it undoubtedly was throughout the year for getting things down from high places, come Christmas lunch it was definitely not the one you wanted to be sitting on. Take your seat too late, and you'd find yourself perched above the fray like a hungry gargoyle on the side of a cathedral.

Then there was the food. But I'll get back to that in a minute.

Since my mother was the first in her large family to get married, my brother was the first child born in the family. I followed just over two years later. The upside of all this, for both me and him, was that come Christmas, having a plethora of aunts and uncles around, we got spoiled when it came to presents.

Mind you, in retrospect, what constituted 'being spoiled' back then probably comes nowhere near the mountain of stuff kids seem to get these days at Christmas as a matter of course. But I would be lying if I didn't make it clear that we did get a lot of presents. However, I can remember hardly any of them. I know that the year after the moon landings we got a pair of walkie-talkie-style phones that were connected to each other by a cable and that we spent most of that Christmas pretending to be Apollo astronauts in one room talking to Ground Control, Houston, in another. (The authentic touch being that at the end of each line you had to say 'beep'.)

Then there was a pair of second-hand bikes that were too big to be wrapped up, so were leant against a wall near the Christmas tree and had a rug thrown over them. The bizarre thing is that I have no recollection of ever having seen them until the moment we got to uncover them. So where my parents had hidden them I have no idea. Then one year there was a clear Perspex game of 3D noughts and crosses. And another year there was a zither that I had pleaded for after having seen one at the house of one of my parents' friends. It must have cost a packet as the zither was such an unusual instrument it was unlikely that anyone made child-sized or toy zithers. I think I played with it for about four days. Then it went back in its box and slowly worked its way to the top of the wardrobe to be ignored for years. I must admit, I feel bad about that now. But I didn't feel bad at the time. After all, it was Christmas.

As the years went by and my aunts and uncles got married and had children of their own, the amount of presents that would turn up at our house on Christmas day had to be seen to be believed. As each new family arrived, their presents would be handed over and placed under the tree to join the others that had spread outwards like a blanket of crocuses in springtime.

The presents would always be opened after Christmas lunch. This is because everyone who was coming would be at the house by lunchtime, and eager though all of us children were to open the presents, the food always came first. Then after the meal, the tables and chairs would be pushed back and all the children would perch excitedly on the floor as the presents were handed out.

My mother would watch as the gifts were received, acknowledged and ripped open with abandon. She would also be clutching a black bin liner to scoop up all the discarded paper. But the paper would only be pushed into the bag once she'd examined it to see if it could be salvaged. If it could, it was carefully folded up and put away somewhere. I suppose it was a legacy of the war years and of being a refugee who had lost everything. Go through that and it's very hard to throw anything away. And, to a certain extent, my mother still acts the same way today. So if anyone out there needs, for instance, a 1997 National Trust calendar, I know where you can get one.

Sometimes my brother and the cousins would 'put on a show'. This would usually involve two or three jokes purloined from the kids' programmes of the day and maybe a song that soon dissolved into mumbles and giggles. But more often than not we'd end up playing with the latest toys, trying to figure out the rules of the games we'd just got, and watching the 'Big Christmas Movie' on TV. This was, of course, when the 'Big Christmas Movie' was something people looked forward to. That's because you could only see films at the cinema when they were released or years later when they finally made it onto TV. Films were much more ephemeral and, somehow, much more important. But they were nowhere near as important to me as they had clearly been to my uncle, my mother's oldest brother.

I have a carefully inscribed notebook of his that assiduously records every single film he saw from 1945 in India, through his family's post-war return to Burma, to his journey to London as the family pioneer in 1950, and all the way up to 1954. In all, he lists, names the stars of and identifies the cinemas that showed 1,340 films. The first film was *Greenwich Village* starring Carmen Miranda and Don Ameche. The last films were a double bill of *Slaughter Trail* and, starring Ray Milland and Grace Kelly, *Dial M For Murder*. The film he saw immediately before his solo arrival in London at the relatively tender age of twenty-one was *On The Town* with Frank Sinatra, which he watched onboard a ship called the *Otranto* as it sailed towards England. The first film he saw on arrival in London was *The Third Man* at the ABC in Clapham, starring Orson Welles. I can't help wondering which of these competing views of big city life struck him as most relevant to understanding the 1950s London he now found himself in. I have a feeling it would have been *The Third Man* – set as it was in war-ravaged Vienna. But I suspect he was hoping that it might have been *On The Town*, with its vibrantly exciting depiction of New York.

The other things we always watched at Christmas were the Christmas specials of our favourite shows. Number one among these was, of course, *Morecambe and Wise*. But every other show also seemed to have a go at a Christmas special. And they would invariably be filled with lame jokes and sideburned guest stars, and feature a carol wedged incongruously somewhere into the mix. Then there was the

Christmas edition of *Top of The Pops*. And back in those days the battle to be the Christmas Number One was not the choreographed farce that it is today. Mind you, back in those days if you wanted to change the channel on the TV, you used to have to get up and walk over to the set and do it by hand.

As the varied collection of people that was my family sat down at the varied collection of tables arranged down the middle of the big room, more food would appear than would make sense. Most of it had been prepared by my parents, but certain significant items were brought in by other people. What was on offer was a glorious collision between the Christmases my mother had grown up with in Burma and India, and the full-on British-style approach.

So there would be roast turkey and stuffing and cranberry sauce and roast potatoes and Brussels sprouts and chipolatas and carrots and gravy and a flaming Christmas pudding with cream or custard and with a sixpence hidden inside it. Then there would be a mountain of subtly spiced rice tinted a vibrant yellow with turmeric, vindaloo made with pork and beef, two chicken curries (one hot, one mild), mulligatawny made with mutton bones, minced meat cutlets (some made with green chillies, some without), lentils, pickled aubergines, raitas, a mixed Burmese salad of cauliflower, carrots and green beans called thanat, beetroot salad, pickles, chutneys and also a salad of tomatoes and cucumber. Then after that there would be traditional semolina-based sweets like the Indian soojee-ka-metha or the Burmese tsunamaki and the small, hard, sugared pastry kul-kuls that the same uncle who had made the cutlets would have stayed up into the early hours churning out.

It was a mountain of food. Or maybe two mountains, one from Asia and one from Europe, which had joined together into a single range. And, tied together by some bond other than rope, my family and friends would successfully reach the summits of both mountains every year. At the end of the meal we would stare down at the land spread out below us and know that all the hard work had been worth it. We had achieved something. We had reached the top.

All that remained was the trek down the mountain, negotiating a scree of clementines and satsumas and bowlfuls of nuts, before we could slump down in the base camp of the sofa and fall asleep in front of the TV.

Beyond the food that undoubtedly provided a common thread through my family's narrative, I primarily remember Christmas as a time of celebration. Games were played. Old songs were sung. Older jokes were told. Just being in the same room as last year, with the same people and answering the same questions (yes, I had grown, and yes, school was OK, and no, I hadn't got a girlfriend) somehow took on a far greater significance than it had any right to. Indeed, if you tried to deconstruct it, all you'd be left with would be little more than a pile of orange peel you didn't get off in one piece, a bin bag full of wrapping paper and a crammed Boxing Day fridge with no room for even a single leftover Brussels sprout. (Shame.)

But a big part of who I am, of who I aspire to be, can be found round the overladen Christmas tables of my childhood. I am that boy with a mad hedge of hair nesting on his head, seriously flared trousers, too much food on his plate, and a smile on his lips as he looks up and sees his family all around him.

However, I still wish that the bike had been new. And that it had been a Chopper.

KUL-KULS
MAKES 137

550g flour
350g fine semolina
1 teaspoon baking powder
½ teaspoon salt
125g butter
6 eggs
125g sugar
1 cup thick coconut milk
2 teaspoons vanilla extract
vegetable oil, for frying
250g sugar and 1½ cups water, for sugaring

Sift together the first four ingredients. Rub in the butter and gently work into the flour and semolina mixture. Separate the eggs. Beat the egg whites into a stiff froth. In a big bowl, add the sugar to the egg yolks and beat into a thick yellow mixture. Add the coconut milk and vanilla extract and the stiffly beaten egg whites. Add the flour and semolina mixture and knead into a soft pliable dough. Form into a ball, smear a little butter over the top, cover with a tea towel and set aside for an hour.

To shape the kul-kuls: grease the prongs of a fork and pinch a piece of dough the size of a large marble. Press the fork into the dough to make ridges, then roll it into a tight curl like a wood shaving. Set it aside on a plate. Form all the dough into these shapes.

Fry the kul-kuls in a pan full of hot oil to a light golden colour. Drain on a paper towel. Leave to cool. When they are cool, melt the extra sugar in the water and cook, uncovered, till one-third of the liquid has evaporated to give a viscous syrup. Drop the kul-kuls into the syrup so that they get evenly coated. Remove with a slotted spoon and transfer to a plate to cool. When cooled, store kul-kuls in an airtight container.

My parents were immigrants. It's a loaded word. It's a negative word. A perennial problem that needs to be addressed. But I look at my family and none of this applies. I'm certain they brought more to this country than they ever took out. I don't think they're part of the problem. I think they're part of the solution. They brought drive, and ambition, and a will to succeed. And, lest we get too carried away with rhetoric here, they brought decent food. I mean, can you imagine how dull food would be in this country without all the wonderful flavours that immigrants have brought with them? God, it would be just like Switzerland. Except the chocolate would be decidedly worse.

As for me, I was born here, so technically I'm not an

immigrant. I'm British. Except I don't feel particularly British. I feel like a Londoner. And more specifically a South Londoner. Admittedly I do live in North London now, but, as we all know, love can make you do crazy things.

What I constantly find surprising, however, is that despite having been born in London and having lived here all my life, I have always felt on the outside of things.

Maybe this explains why, of the hundreds of books I've read, one of the very few passages that has stayed with me is this one from *The Wind in the Willows* by Kenneth Grahame. Rat and Mole are making their way home through a village one winter's night.

> The rapid nightfall of mid-December had quite beset the little village as they approached it on soft feet over a first thin fall of powdery snow. Little was visible but squares of a dusky orange-red on either side of the street, where the firelight or lamplight of each cottage overflowed through the casements into the dark world without. Most of the low latticed windows were innocent of blinds, and to the lookers-in from outside, the inmates, gathered round the tea-table, absorbed in handiwork, or talking with laughter and gesture, had each that happy grace which is the last thing the skilled actor shall capture – the natural grace which goes with perfect unconsciousness of observation. Moving at will from one theatre to another, the two spectators, so far from home themselves, had something of wistfulness in their eyes as they watched

a cat being stroked, a sleepy child picked up and huddled off to bed, or a tired man stretch and knock out his pipe on the end of a smouldering log.

Given that my own family life was a happy and close-knit one, it is an odd passage of writing with which to relate. But I do. Whatever I do, wherever I go, a part of me always feels out in the snow with my face pressed up against a window. I'd always put it down to being the child of immigrants. To having a brown skin in a predominantly white world. To not even being part of the mainstream British Asian community. But when I started to delve into my father's story I discovered another possible explanation as to why I've always felt on the outside. That's because he did too. Even in Ceylon, the country he grew up in.

Genetics is a strange thing. And I don't think we're even close to fully understanding it. Yes, we know that we can inherit physical features, intellectual capabilities, even some aspects of personality, but I've never seen it recorded anywhere that we can inherit feelings. But I think that maybe I did. I think I inherited the feeling of always being on the outside looking in. And as I stood outside in the snow, looking in through the window, if only I'd turned my head to one side I'd have seen my father standing next to me.

six

CEYLON

About the only person still around who knew my father when he was a young man is my godfather. They had been friends in the late 1940s in Ceylon and they both travelled to London in the early 1950s, where they shared digs and then moved into a flat together. My memories of my godfather are slight, as he had moved back to Ceylon to practise architecture when I was still very small, then went on to America to teach. There were cards on my birthday, a rare voice on the end of the phone and one fleeting visit to London, of which all I can remember is the photograph of the two of us taken in the back garden, in which I stand an awkward and diffident and tubby teenager with too much hair and too little jumper. Now he was living just outside Boston, where he had retired from his job teaching architecture at the university. And I hadn't seen him for almost thirty years.

I got his phone number from my mother.

'Hello, Valentine, this is Rohan, how are you?'

'Fine, fine, son, how are you? How is your mother keeping?'

'I'm well. My mum's well. Or she is now. Last year there were a few problems. But she's much better.'

'So, Rohan, when are you coming to see me?'

It was a question he always asked every time I spoke to him.

'How about two weeks' time?'

My father was born in Colombo, Ceylon, in 1929. I'm not sure what his father did. The only stories I can track down suggest that he was a bit of a wheeler-dealer. He was always a man with a scheme. He liked to dress well. And he was fond of a flutter. He had four children, one of whom died as a baby. My father was the middle one of the three who survived. But soon after the last child was born, his wife also died. And that, apparently, knocked him for six. He couldn't cope.

Luckily for him, luckily for my father, indeed luckily for all of us, his sister took them all in hand. My father remembered playing in the dust outside his house one day when his aunt arrived and asked why he wasn't in school. He didn't have a good answer. That's when his aunt decided to take charge of things. She took her brother's children into her home and created an environment in which they could grow. It must have been a very crowded place, as she had also taken in her sister, who had two young daughters and whose husband had died. What's more, she was bringing up her own young son by herself because her husband had left to go to India to be a painter. By all accounts it was a strict household. But given the circumstances it probably needed to be. There were too many mouths to feed, too many children to raise and too little money coming in to do it any other way. To make ends meet, my father's aunt taught Tamil, Sinhala and English to the children of richer families who would come to her home each day. There was love and laughter in the house, too, and my father's aunt encouraged and inspired the children in many ways.

In pictures of the aunt that I've seen, her salt and pepper hair is always pulled tightly back. She doesn't smile. Her glazed, distracted eyes seem to suggest that she's thinking that having your picture taken is a foolish waste of time in a world where there's just too much to do. She looks worn down by life. When her own son was twenty-one he went off to the dentist for some fairly minor work and never came back. He died in the dentist's chair. They never found out why.

My father had always struck me as a man at ease with both himself and the world. He seemed to know who he was and to be content to find his own path through the forest. There was nothing in anything he did, or said, or how he lived his life, to suggest that he harboured any hurt or anger or bitterness. But, apparently, he did. At least, that's what my godfather explained. He hesitated over the word 'bitterness', but in the end decided that it was the right one. When I came back from Boston and asked my mother about this, she confirmed that there had been an anger in my father. It might have slipped further and further back into his personality as he grew older, but it was there.

It stemmed from the fact that my father's relatives, beyond his immediate family, were pretty well off. They all came from a community, generations ago from India, called Chettiars. Variously described as being traders, moneylenders and landlords, they were a caste of people usually associated with financial success. Not that many of them were traders, moneylenders or landlords any more. And the caste system, while not being as rigid and all-embracing as it was in parts of India, was still important.

The problem for my father was that his own father had slipped through the cracks. He had lost his place at the top table and was grubbing around trying to make a living as best he could. He had let the side down. He, and his children, were a bit of an embarrassment. Now my father, when I knew him, was a clever man. And I bet that as a child he was exactly the same. He would have known what was going on. He would have seen how he, and his brother and sister, and his father, were being treated. While as a child he might not have been in a position to do anything about it, he would have soaked up the slights and the subtle rejections and internalised the feelings of injustice that would inevitably accrue.

All this was news to me. Ask any of the people who knew him after he came to England and I bet not a single one would have detected even a hint of bitterness in his character. But somewhere, buried deep down, it was there.

The only tangible example I have of how it worked is a story he told my mother, and which she in turn told me. Somewhat inevitably it all came down to food. My father could remember as a small child being included with his brother and sister in celebrations that his extended family members would hold. They would be invited, presumably because the social code of that particular group at that particular time decreed that this was the right thing to do. While they may have been invited, they weren't made welcome. So he could remember, while the festivities were going on in another part of the building with the best of everything, that he would have to sit in the kitchen with the cooks eating the third class of rice. Rice that you had to pick husks and small stones from before you could eat. And young though he was, he no doubt got the message.

On top of that you have to remember that this was Ceylon in the 1930s. The country was still firmly a part of the British Empire. What this meant was that the place was subject to two overlapping hierarchies. First there was the British colonial system with all the layers and constructs that came with it. Then there was the indigenous class and caste system. My father, as he grew up, was outside both. One he had no access to because he wasn't British. The other he was rejected by because his father had 'let the side down'. On top of all that, after his mother died, he never had the chance to grow up within a conventional family structure.

No wonder he chose to make his own way in the world.

My father never said much about his early life, but my mother tells a story that quietly hints at what must have been a vast ocean of loss. It comes from the time after he and my mother married and he was having difficulty settling on what to call his new mother-in-law.

'Why don't you call her Mum?' my mother asked.

My father paused. And then he said, 'I've never called anyone Mum. I can't start now.'

A small handful of words can reveal so much. But it's the pause that makes me feel for him the most. What was he thinking in that brief, fleeting moment?

When he did get married he built a family life as solid as Sigiriya. What he never had, he made sure we got. And just writing these words I begin to understand something about him that I never did before. One of the things he did soon after he came to England was to start painting pictures. Bold, uncompromising, abstract pictures. And he was, to my admittedly biased eye at least, very good. But he never seemed to pursue the world of art as seriously as his talent warranted. Maybe that's because if you choose the path of an artist, and an artist who paints obscure abstractions in a largely indifferent 1950s Britain, and pursue it uncompromisingly, then the chances of creating a stable and secure family environment get chucked out of the window with the squeezed-out tubes of paint.

However, all this lies years in the future. At the moment he's still growing up in Ceylon, trying to figure out his place in the world, trying to decide who he's going to be.

But of his early years I know very little more. There is only that one picture of him as a child, the one where he is a boy scout. Over the years I have stared at it for a long time. But all I see is a boy staring back.

When my plane landed in Boston it was into a snowstorm. Fat white flakes were driven by the wind horizontally past the windows of the plane as it taxied to its berth at the terminal. Waiting for my bags to appear on the carousel, I wondered whether my godfather would recognise me. And would I recognise him? And, more importantly, would we be able to talk to each other beyond the first exchange of pleasantries and family news?

As I came through the arrivals gate it was not Valentine who was waiting for me but Ranee his wife, my godmother. She was a small woman, in a big coat, with a smile that lit up her whole face. Valentine, she said, was outside with the car. I followed her out, dragging my case behind me. Their car was far from new and sat low in the kerbside slush. Valentine was behind the wheel, bundled up in a quilted coat and thick gloves with a flat cap perched on his head. He greeted me with a warmth that made me feel as if I'd come home.

The drive from the airport was slow and treacherous. The windscreen wipers vainly sweeping snow away only for it to build up again instantly. The car occasionally slid side-ways on the slush-covered ice. Getting off the highway and onto a slip road was no easy task. Once away from the main road we drove through snow-muffled trees and past large

New England clapboard houses, any one of which could have made a respectable postcard. My godfather's house, when we reached it, was a much smaller affair, but in its own modest way just as idyllic.

Six inches of snow fell that night. And when, the next morning, I asked my godfather how long there'd been snow on the ground, he said they'd had it since November. And this was March. But once we'd exchanged family news, and pored over the latest photographs, and I'd handed over the small gifts my mother had packed, we got down to the purpose of my visit. And when my godfather started talking about the Ceylon he remembered from sixty years ago, the snow piled high outside the windows soon disappeared.

He talked about the heat of the sun as he walked home from school in his white cotton shirt. The juice of a ripe mango as it dripped down his chin. And the flash of the wings of a golden oriole as it swooped down from the branches of a palm tree. The light in his eyes as he spoke revealed the much younger man that was still within him, still on the parched cricket fields of his youth, still elegantly stroking a cover drive for four.

When the Second World War came in 1939, my father was ten years old. Although people like my father and godfather were far from the action, they were clear where they stood. They stood with the British. After all, they spoke English. They had been educated in British-style schools. My father had even been raised attending an Anglican church every Sunday. Britain was a key part of the context in which they framed their identity.

I asked my godfather whether there weren't any split in loyalties. After all, didn't they want an end to colonialism? Didn't they want the British to leave Ceylon? Didn't they crave independence from the empire?

My godfather replied that of course they deeply longed for all of these things, but the war was different. They saw it in simple black and white terms. It was a struggle between good and evil. And as Hitler's armies marched across Europe towards the English Channel, the British were seen as the outnumbered heroes with their backs against the wall.

There was also a real fear of the Japanese, who seemed to be progressing irresistibly across Southeast Asia. As it turned out, they never made it as far as Ceylon. But they did try. Churchill, apparently, described it as 'the most dangerous moment' of the Second World War. Singapore had already fallen, and if Ceylon had followed, the Japanese would have had a base from which to attack India. Then, in control of both the Far East and Southeast Asia, they would have been only a short step away from joining up with the Axis powers in North Africa.

The man most credited with interrupting this domino fall was a Canadian, Squadron Leader Len Birchall. In March 1942 he'd been serving on the Shetland Islands. On the second of April 1942 he arrived in Ceylon. Two days later he was flying his first reconnaissance mission in an unarmed Catalina flying boat. At the end of a long patrol, just as the plane was about to turn for home, he spotted a small black speck on the horizon. Despite being low on fuel he turned to investigate. The 'speck' turned out to be the full might of the

Japanese fleet sailing towards what they hoped would be a Pearl Harbor-style appointment with Ceylon.

The Japanese launched a gang of Zero fighters to take down the defenceless Catalina. And they succeeded. But not before Birchall had got a signal off, warning of the impending attack. The Catalina, riddled with bullets, crash-landed into the sea. Birchall was hauled aboard one of the Japanese destroyers. He remembers being repeatedly beaten as a senior officer, using perfect English, asked the vital question, 'Did you send a message?' He had just convinced them that no message had been sent when the Japanese intercepted a transmission from the base at Colombo asking him to repeat his warning.

He spent the rest of the war in a succession of Japanese prison camps. But his message had alerted the British in Ceylon to the approach of the Japanese. With the element of surprise gone, the Japanese limited their assault on the island to a couple of half-hearted bombing raids. But if Squadron Leader Len Birchall had been looking the other way on that last leg of his first, and last, reconnaissance flight, things might have been very different.

It's hardly surprising then that the war, both in Europe and in the Far Eastern theatre, was followed so closely in Ceylon. Radio bulletins were religiously tuned in to, and maps marking the advances of the enemy were pinned to countless walls. The world was in flux and small though Ceylon was, it was hard not to be caught up in the events that had turned the whole globe into one story with a single, compelling narrative.

Towards the end of the conflict my father tried to join the Fleet Air Arm, but they told him that he was too young. By the time he was old enough to enrol, the war had ended. The British had won and good had triumphed over evil. So there was no need to join up to fight. Instead my father signed on to train as a civilian draughtsman with the Navy. When he had completed his qualifications and had served out his time, he left to get a job with a civilian company. The best architectural practice in Colombo at the time was a British firm called Edwards, Reid & Begg. Because of the training he had received, and an obvious natural ability, he walked into a job as a draughtsman with no problems. It was while he was working there that he first met my godfather, who was put under my father's wing when he joined.

My godfather looked up to my father and soon recognised that he was the best draughtsman in the firm. Early on in their time working together, they were given the task of surveying the hillside of a tea plantation where the land was to be cleared to build the best possible accommodation for the local plantation workers. The project involved living on site up in the hills for almost three months. It was a rare opportunity for both of them to be in charge of the early stage of a project and it was a job they took to with relish. If nothing else it gave them the chance to live away from home and to spend the long, warm evenings talking about everything under the sun. They found, among other things, that they were kindred spirits.

Like my father, my godfather came from a family that once had money but had fallen on harder times. So both of them had long been on the outside looking in. As their friendship grew they talked about politics and religion, and cricket and the arts. One enduring debate that my godfather remembers concerned whether the superior recording of Beethoven's Ninth Symphony was the one by Furtwängler or the one by Toscanini.

When I think about the debates I had about the arts at a similar age, I can't help feeling like an uncultured fool. For me it would have been, 'Why haven't I been able to get into *Twin Peaks*?' Or: 'Have Madness lost their magic now that they've gone all serious?' And I don't think I ever had a real discussion about politics, not even at university. I did go on the marches, however, but that's just what students did back then. Mind you, I do now own a recording of Beethoven's Ninth. It's just that I never listen to it.

The picture on the back cover of this book of a man holding a rose comes from this time. It's my father, and my godfather took the shot. So I have a few fading photos of their time at the tea plantation. Among them is a picture that had always puzzled me until I showed it to my godfather in snowbound Boston. In it, the two laughing friends stand against a washed-out horizon, but the shot's spoiled by a thin knobbly branch of wood that starts in a blur in the top right-hand corner of the picture, then angles in to the figures in the middle. When my godfather saw the picture he started to laugh, saying he had never seen it before but he remembered precisely the moment when it was taken. It was one morning before they had started work. They'd taken pictures of each other, but now they wanted one of the two of them together. The only problem was that there was no one around to ask. So they set the camera on a flat rock, focused the lens to a set distance, then found the longest stick they could and, standing back from the camera, used the carefully extended stick to gently tap the shutter release. Sixty years later my godfather discovered for the first time that the plan had worked. The picture may have started to fade, but the memory hadn't. He was laughing again. Only this time it was with me and not my father.

One thing that soon became clear to them, whether at the tea plantation or later, was that their futures did not lie in Ceylon. The war had done many things. Primary among these was to shatter the illusion that the old order was set in stone. No one believed that any more. Even those who clung to the age-old certainties that it seemed to embody knew that change was coming. Britain might have won the war, but, exhausted, it realised that the days of empire were rapidly drawing to a close. No one had a real appetite to hang onto colonies that were pressing, with varying degrees of vigour, to cut the ties of serfdom to Britain.

Just as nations were realising that change was not only possible, but also probable, so too were people. In many ways for my father and godfather, Ceylon at that moment should have held the promise of all kinds of future success. The problem was that even as the old colonial hierarchy was packing up its belongings and metaphorically deciding whether an elephant's foot umbrella-stand would really fit into a modest bungalow in Pinner, another hierarchy was ready and waiting to step in and take its place.

Every liberation movement, having succeeded in overthrowing the old order, finds it necessary to impose a new order in its place. While more often than not they are better than what preceded them, they are still, nonetheless, a hierarchy that holds power. Now, if you're outside that hierarchy, while many things will no doubt change for you under the new regime, one thing often remains resolutely the same. You're on the outside looking in. And that's the position that my father and godfather could both see lay ahead of them as Ceylon moved towards independence.

They saw Ceylon as heading to a bright new future where old school ties, family connections and which clubs you belonged to still played a major part in your chances of getting on. It was just that the colour of the skin of the people in the clubs, with the right family connections and wearing the old school ties, had changed. While my father and godfather may have had the right coloured skin, what they lacked were the right connections.

In saying that, I am no doubt maligning many of those who worked for independence for far simpler and nobler reasons, but this is the way that the two friends saw things. But they also saw what the war had taught everyone, namely that change was possible. And if the change they wanted couldn't be found at home, then they'd save their money, get on board a boat and sail off to find a bright new horizon.

My godfather set off for England first, in 1952. My father followed the next year.

* * *

Crowded though the house my father grew up in was, there was always enough to eat. Ceylon is a lush country where food has always been available in abundance and where the diverse ethnic groups that have visited the island over the centuries have all contributed to a rich cuisine. While supplies were somewhat limited during the war, and the daily fare was often pretty simple, there would still be occasional treats to excite the palate.

So over the years my father ate an incredibly wide range of delicious food. There would have been chicken curries (at least four kinds), beef curries, pork curries and mutton curries. A dry pickled fish curry called ambuthiyal with a characteristic black colour and the distinctive flavouring of goraka. Numerous other fish curries too, and then curried crabs (with different spicings for each type of crab), and prawn curries made with prawns as fat as your thumbs.

Sometimes the different curries were simply classified by whether they were 'red' or 'black' – the black ones tending to be drier and featuring spices that had first been dry-roasted in a pan to intensify the flavours. The Muslim influence could be seen in the popularity of rich aromatic birianis of lamb or chicken.

Vegetables would also be cooked in a myriad of styles, but currying ruled supreme. Pumpkins, bitter gourds, jackfruits, sweet potatoes, aubergines, snake beans, tomatoes, pineapples and cashew nuts all made excellent curries. I've even come across a recipe for omelette curry, described as a very Ceylonese invention.

Rice would be cooked in a variety of ways, perhaps the

most significant being kiribath – coconut rice – traditionally the first solid food given to a baby, and also served at weddings. Iddiappam, a dish made from rice-flour vermicelli, was also often served on festive occasions.

Flat breads and pancakes came in many forms. There would be parathas, rotis, pooris, nans and European-style loaves, which were much appreciated for their ability to soak up curry gravies. Then there were hoppers, crispy bowl-shaped rice-flour pancakes popular at breakfast, lunch or dinner. They are traditional street-vendor food and come in varieties that can be either savoury or sweet, or just plain when used to mop up curries. Egghoppers are another favourite variation and feature (unsurprisingly) an egg nestling in the bottom of the bowl-shaped pancake. Stringhoppers were much loved, too, made from a Chinese rice-flour dough extruded through special moulds and then stacked up in a steamer and cooked.

Sambols were compulsory, a sambol being a relish, eaten relatively fresh, that sits somewhere between a pickle and a chutney and is served as an accompaniment to a meal of rice and curry. Lunu miris – hot onion sambol – was made with dried chillies, onion and dried Maldive fish. Seeni sambol was a variation on this, featuring caramelised onions and a touch of sugar. Pol sambol, made with coconut, was almost a national dish. And acharoo – a mixed vegetable pickle – gave a refreshing crunch to many a meal.

To satisfy the sweet tooth there was kiri-pan. This was buffalo milk curd served with a treacle made by reducing down jaggery – the local, smokily intense, brown palm sugar. Also traditional were the deliciously sticky, spicy, coconut-based bibikkan, and the moist and rich love cake, another popular wedding treat. Love cake is a clear legacy of centuries of European colonisation, as cake-making is not part of the indigenous cuisine.

But my father's favourite pudding was wattalappan. Made with both jaggery and coconut – two of the most distinctive flavours in the Ceylonese kitchen – its nearest equivalent is a steamed egg custard. But while that might be a near equivalent, believe me it doesn't really come close. The following is my godmother's recipe for wattalappan. Just don't let her know that I shared it with you.

WATTALAPPAN
SERVES 5

8oz jaggery
8 tablespoons water
5 eggs
1 tin coconut milk
1 teaspoon grated nutmeg
2 tablespoons raisins
2 tablespoons sliced cashew nuts

Put the jaggery in a pan with half the water. Bring to the boil, then simmer until the jaggery has dissolved. Allow to cool. Beat the eggs well and add to the jaggery. Add the coconut milk and mix well. Stir in the nutmeg. Put a few raisins and cashew nuts into the bottom of a bowl and strain the liquid over it (so that no lumps of jaggery or egg go in). Cover the bowl with greaseproof paper and place in a pan of simmering water for about 40 minutes or until firm. Alternatively, place the covered bowl in a steamer and steam till firm. Allow to cool, then chill in the refrigerator. Serve chilled. (Throw the other half of the water away.)

The food at McCoy's Guest House, near Ecclestone Square in Victoria, must have come as a quite considerable shock to the system. It was March 1953, and my father's first meal was spam, prised from a tin, served with a choice of over-boiled vegetables. And that was only available after he'd handed over his ration book to Mary McCoy, who ran the digs. Getting the ration book in the first place had involved a freezing trek to the Home Office to present his student visa. A trip that was the very first thing he did once he'd turned up at McCoy's, because if he didn't have a ration book he wouldn't have got any food.

The only memory of his boat trip to Britain on the *Otranto* that my father ever talked about involved dinner one night when steak was served. He remembers picking up the salt cellar and sprinkling 'salt' liberally over the steak. The other passengers at his table watched, fascinated, as he took his first bite. He had, in fact, covered the meat in sugar. My father, not wanting to appear a fool, assiduously chewed all the way through his sweetened sirloin, insisting as he did so that this was how he always ate it.

Leaving Colombo had been a big deal. There had been a huge send-off. Back then, sailing halfway around the world was like a trip to the moon. When he set sail with the aim of studying architecture in London, he knew he would be gone for at least five years. And, after that, who knew where he would go and when, if ever, he would come back. He looked at the people who had come to the jetty to see him off and realised that there were probably friends and relatives among them he would never see again.

The trip took thirty-one days, and cost a savings-account-decimating sixty-seven pounds. That was for a cabin below the waterline, shared with three others. The boat stopped at Aden, Port Said, Naples, Marseilles and Gibraltar before finally arriving in Tilbury. His first impression of Tilbury, the docks and the Thames, was one of disappointment. He was horrified by what he saw as the lack of structural order. But he'd forgotten that this was not long after the war. Many of the places he saw had been bombed and it would be years before they really picked themselves up again.

London itself, despite the ample evidence of the severity of the Blitz it had endured, offered something like order. The house that my father stayed at was part of a terrace of down-at-heel, tall Georgian properties. Too big for the single families that once could afford to live in them, many had been converted into flats or boarding houses. Now they housed a diverse mixture of students and workers who had made their way to London in search of – if not necessarily their fortune then at least – work. In the days when a policy of 'No Blacks, No Dogs, No Irish' was still widespread, the McCoys made everyone welcome. Accordingly, my father found himself in a house with lots of Irish, a couple of

Africans and quite a few Ceylonese. One of the Ceylonese was my godfather, who had been at the house since his arrival the year before.

My godfather had an eight-foot by sixteen-foot room on the first floor, with a grimy Georgian window that looked out onto the blank, lifeless eyes of the windows across the street. My father had a smaller room that, because it was up another two flights of stairs, was cheaper. These small, bare rooms were home for them for the next two years.

London, even several years after the end of the war, was still a city in the early stages of recovery. The euphoria that had immediately followed the victory had long since been replaced by a realisation that the country was skint, knackered and in need of rebuilding. And the capital needed more rebuilding than most. For my father this last fact was a godsend. That's because even though he had come to Britain in order to study to become a fully qualified architect, he'd spent all the money he had managed to save over the years just to buy the ticket for the journey. If he was going to be able to pay for his studies, he'd first have to get work to support himself. As a fully trained and an experienced draughtsman in a city that had been blitzed, finding work was not a problem. Everywhere you looked, new buildings needed to be built or old buildings repaired. Within the first couple of weeks of arriving in London, he found employment and he never stopped working. What I've only just discovered is that because he never stopped working, he never had the time to study. So he never officially qualified as an architect.

For me, this was a revelation. All my life I had thought that he was an architect. But while he probably had all the knowledge and experience to not only be one, but a good one, he never actually had the qualifications. I'm not at all sure how significant this is, but I must admit that when I discovered it I did feel a little disorientated. I have no idea why this should be. After all, he was still the same person he had always been, still the same father, it was just that he wasn't, officially, an architect. He was an architectural assistant.

One evening when we were talking in Boston my godfather dropped another revelation into the conversation.

We were discussing the other food he remembered eating at McCoy's. He recalled a multitude of Irish stews, more spam, occasionally cheap cuts of beef roasted, pies, porridge for breakfast with, at the weekend, eggs and bacon cut on a slicer, also cabbage and a mountain of boiled potatoes – after all, the McCoys were Irish. For puddings he remembered stewed tinned gooseberries. But looming large in his recollections was creamy yellow blancmange, dished up in large enamel washing-up bowls. The food was served by Irish waitresses in the dining room downstairs below ground level where, because there wasn't enough room for everyone, guests would eat in rotation.

In the middle of this reminiscing my godfather mentioned the literary magazine that my father had started.

What?

This was so unexpected an aside that I was certain my godfather must have been misrepresenting or misremembering something from all those years ago. When I pressed him on the subject he couldn't recall much else. Back in London I asked my mother about it. She said yes, it was true. And a couple of days later she had dug out two copies of the magazine for me to look at.

It was called *New Chapter – A Quarterly Magazine of Literature*. My father edited it with someone called Robert Bruce. Volume 1 Number 1 was published in May 1957 and featured, in its own words, 'Fiction-Travel-Drama-Poetry'.

The editorial in the first issue focused in terms I have great difficulty following on the merits of the 'Movement', a school of poetry in vogue at the time through the work of Philip Larkin and Kingsley Amis, which was famed for its 'metaphysical wit, its glittering intellectuality, its rich Empsonian ambiguities'.

No. I have no idea what an 'Empsonian ambiguity' is either. Let alone a rich one.

New Chapter wanted to plough a far wider furrow. 'Diversity is the subject mark of the prose we publish. All in all we hope to have succeeded in bringing out a magazine of literature which is catholic in nature and high in quality, and which may in part help diffuse the spotlight on the Movement and light up the whole of the stage of poetry today.'

The first volume contained a variety of poems, including one by Elizabeth Jennings, a short story that begins 'The wardrobe had come to Seymour from Aunt Trix', a piece of travel writing set aboard a steamer going upriver in British Guiana, and a very critical examination of the 'Method' school of acting as a way of performing Shakespeare. The only other volume I have came out in September 1958 and features a nicely critical view of Samuel Beckett's *Endgame* that concludes:

> Well, there it is. Either you yourself despair, and think that *Endgame* is a vision of truth; or you have faith and hope and think, as I do, that Beckett's play is amusing and well done, but too slight in every respect to be considered as great drama. If you neither despair nor hope, but like *Endgame* because liking it goes with black jeans and a girlfriend with coal dust round the eyes and no lipstick, I am afraid you are, as Beckett might say, a *clodd*.

So in little over four years after getting off the boat with next to nothing in his pocket, my father was launching and editing a literary magazine taking on the likes of Beckett, Larkin and indeed Brando, and trying to establish himself as a painter of obscure abstractions, all the while holding down a full-time job. No wonder he never qualified as an architect. He just didn't have the time.

On top of all this somewhere along the line he met, and fell for, my mother.

One of the other things that my godfather vividly remembers about his first year in Britain was the weather. He had arrived in London in the February of 1952. My father came the following March. And it was cold. Very cold. In all their life in Ceylon neither of them had ever been cold. Snow, a joy on first sight seen through a window, soon revealed its true nature once you got out into it and its freezing wetness started to soak through your clothes and your recently bought heavy shoes. Fogs descended onto the capital with very little warning. And because these were still the days when many homes were heated by coal, and air pollution was unchecked, the fogs often thickened into smogs. My godfather remembers days when buses were cancelled and men walked the pavements with flares held out to light their way. Some days your world was cut down to three yards in front of you. It would become oppressively claustrophobic and everyone would walk round with their handkerchiefs held firmly over their mouths and noses. By the end of the day the handkerchiefs would be black with soot.

It was all a world away from the blue skies and clear air of the land that he and my father had grown up in. Unfortunately, my father didn't help the state of his lungs by smoking Players Senior Service cigarettes. Many years later he switched to the occasional cigar, but I still have very clear memories of those white cigarette boxes with their sailor logo. To this day I can see his strong tapering fingers, the nail ends stained a dirty yellow by the nicotine.

In the years that I knew him, whenever the winter weather got the better of him and he succumbed to a cold, my father fought back with an age-old Ceylonese recipe. If chicken soup is the Jewish antibiotic, then rasam was the equivalent for my father. One bowlful of that and even the most vicious of colds would soon be cowering in the corner of the room pleading for mercy. Rasam is often called pepper water, but that innocuous title hardly does it justice. Fire water would be a far more appropriate name. And when a cold struck my father he would stand, woolly-capped, in the kitchen concocting a brew potent enough to defeat all comers. Whenever I had a cold, I'd get some too. And I'm still not entirely certain that I've completely recovered from the cure to this day.

The recipe I give you below should be treated with caution. You should only really attempt it after you've already been given the last rites. It is the only soup known to man able to cut its way through a 1950s London smog.

RASAM
SERVES 4

6 teaspoons tamarind extract
3 tablespoons oil
1 teaspoon mustard seeds
4 cloves garlic, finely sliced
1 teaspoon peppercorns
1½ teaspoons turmeric powder
2 teaspoons cumin powder
1½ teaspoons chilli powder
2 teaspoons salt
3 onions, finely sliced
4 dried red chillies
6 curry leaves

Mix the tamarind with 2 pints hot water.

Heat the oil in a saucepan, add half the mustard seeds, half the garlic, the peppercorns, turmeric, cumin and chilli powder. Fry gently for 1 minute. Add the tamarind juice and salt. Leave to simmer.

In frying pan, fry the onions (don't brown), the remaining garlic and mustard seeds and the red chillies. Add the curry leaves, stir, then add the fried ingredients to the saucepan. Simmer for 10–15 minutes.

Taste.

Spend the rest of the day searching for the top of your head.

seven

A MANGOSTEEN IN THE
APPLE TREE

Investigate your past and one thought you inevitably find
yourself unable to escape is that everything could have been
so different, so very easily.

Think about it for any length of time and you can find
yourself starting to believe in either fate or God. Otherwise,
the more you look into it, the more you're confronted by
the likelihood that you are where you are courtesy of the
randomness of life.

If your grandfather had turned left, not right, that
day he would never have met your grandmother. If
the Japanese planes hadn't wheeled away the boat would
have been sunk and the family would never have
escaped. If the man who was interviewing you hadn't
had a 'good lunch' he wouldn't have laughed at your
feeble jokes, so you wouldn't have got your first job in

advertising and you would have ended up programming computers.

And what if your mother had married someone else? Then your father would not have been your father. And you would not have been you. More worryingly, 'you' would not have been anyone.

All this comes to mind because, it turns out, my mother left a string of broken hearts across two continents. For a very long time, one of the broken hearts she left was her own.

She was, it has to be said, a very beautiful young woman. And clever. And funny. And, of course, I am outrageously biased. But when I discovered the list of would-be suitors she left staring wistfully into the distance, I can only conclude that I wasn't the first person to be swayed by her charms.

Her career as a veritable Helen of Vypeen, Rangoon and Thornton Heath, South London, really took off on the Indian island where her family fled from the invading Japanese during the war. The Vypeen Catholic community was a small one. Everyone knew everyone. And almost everyone was, in some long lost way, related to almost everyone else. It was a happy, thriving, vibrant community. If you were born and grew up on the island, the chances were that you would marry someone from the island. Unless, of course, you left to make your fortune in the outside world. But even if you did, there was always the strong possibility that you would return to the island to marry your childhood sweetheart.

My mother lived on Vypeen from the age of eleven to the age of sixteen. Ample time to be a childhood sweetheart. And to be a fiancée.

My mother would probably prefer it if I didn't go through a list of her admirers. But, to be honest, I'm not doing it for her. I'm doing it for my aunt. The aunt who was ill on the boat and who was nearest in age to my mum. Because they were sisters, and close in age, they shared everything as they grew up. Experiences, friendships, hopes, fears and dreams. Not long after my mum got married, my aunt did too, and moved to Malaysia, her husband's home. But at any time in her life my mother could pick up the phone and know that at the other end of it would be someone who knew her. Really knew her. And my aunt felt the same.

A year ago, me and my mother flew out to Malacca to spend some time with my aunt because she was in the last stages of a dance with cancer. Seeing her on this trip was very difficult for my mum. While I had been growing up, although my mother may have been beautiful, my aunt was stunning. I remember her as always being immaculately turned out, such as in an elegantly beautiful orchid-print dress, with flowers perfectly pinned in her hair. But by the time we arrived in Malacca my aunt's cancer had claimed its pound of flesh. And then it had claimed a whole lot more. Needless to say she was still as elegantly turned out as ever. But she was skin and bone. Except somehow she was far, far more than that. When she spoke it was with a life force that was vibrant, aware and undeniable. She had accepted her situation, but had not given in to it. Flying out to see her, I had been troubled. I didn't know what to expect. I didn't know how to react. But within the first ten minutes of being with my aunt I realised that I had no right to feel sorry for her, because she didn't feel sorry for herself. She was just getting on with living as much life as she had left.

My mother found the situation harder to come to terms with. No doubt, flying out, she knew that this would be the last time she'd see her sister. But it was only when she sat down with her, a sister who'd get exhausted by the slightest exertion, who could eat what seemed to be less than a hummingbird sipping nectar from a flower, whose face was sunken and drawn almost out of all recognition, did the physical finality of what lay ahead become real.

It's hard to say goodbye to someone you love. So you don't say goodbye. You spend as much time as you can with them. You savour every second. You pore over every shared memory. You renew the bonds that, as you were growing up going through so much together, you never thought would ever be broken. You recall the faces, you grope for the names, you feel the sun that used to shine on you both, you taste the flavours, you smell the flowers, you stumble along the now overgrown paths that were once so familiar and well worn, and you laugh. You laugh a lot. Because you laughed so much when you were young. In truth, you're still young. It's just that your bodies have got old. And you can't figure out how that happened.

I was lucky to have the chance to spend this time with my aunt and my mother. I felt privileged. I would never have imagined that going to see someone who was, in effect, dying could have been a life-affirming experience, but it was. When I flew back I felt sad, I felt happy and I felt uplifted. Which was a feeling I had never expected to have.

All this about my mother's ex-admirers is really for my aunt. Because as she regaled us with a rundown on all her older sister's beaus, she would be almost crying with laughter. My mum would be laughing, too, berating her sister for letting her son know all about her chequered past.

Barbara, wherever you are, I'm putting this in just for you. After all, why should the fact that you're dead prevent you from teasing your elder sister one last time? And the great thing is, she can't get you back.

First up there was H. He met, and fell in love with, my mother when she was sixteen. He worked for the British Army. Then, when he was demobbed, he went to the Middle East to make his 'fortune'. He was a canny business-man and he did well. He came back to Vypeen to find my mother had gone back to Burma. So, after a while, he went to Burma. Only to find that by now my mother's family had gone to England. So he travelled to England, but couldn't track them down. He returned to the island, heartbroken. Many years later, in the 1990s, my aunt met him again. That's when he told her that my mother had been the love of his life.

Next came I. He was a bandleader from Cochin on the Indian mainland. Cochin was famous for its musicians in those days. He and his band had been invited to play at a wedding on the island. He spotted my mother and was obviously very taken with her. After a while he was ready to propose. But my mother said no.

After H and I came J. (At which point in my aunt's recounting of the course of events I started to get the distinct impression that my mother was working her way through the alphabet.) But these were far more innocent times. Infatuations never really got much further than fluttering eyelashes in church of a Sunday, or furtive glances across a crowded market. J was a ship's officer at the time. He, too, was ready to propose. But my mother wasn't ready to accept. Or even to be asked yet.

When the family returned to Rangoon after the war to try to restart their old life, my mother was wooed by DD. He lived on the next block. He was very dapper. He wore long-sleeved Shanghai silk shirts, snakeskin trousers and suede shoes. He worked for the port commissioner. At his sister's wedding, at which my mother was a bridesmaid, he did propose. At which point my mum made her excuses and left.

Next there were, what my aunt dubbed, the Three Musketeers. These were three friends who always went around together. All three of them wanted to go out with my mother. So they did. All together. They decided to let her choose who was to be the lucky one. (Which kind of makes it sound like a very early version of *Blind Date*. But obviously without the tacky questions.)

Unfortunately for the Three Musketeers, my mum had already chosen. And it wasn't to be any of them. It was P. Thirteen years older than she was, sophisticated, cultured, elegant. He played the piano, wrote music and was the science master at the school. He dressed only in black and white. And his emotions were as clear-cut as his sense of style. He fell in love with my mother. And she fell in love with him.

All was going well, until my grandparents decided that the family's future lay halfway around the world in England. My mother, by now twenty-two, didn't want to go. Her life, and her love, were in Burma. Eventually my grandmother talked her round. She reasoned that if the family were to get established in England they would need all the help they could get. My mum, if she went with them, would be able to work. Frankly, the family would need the money she could bring in. Especially as so many of my mother's brothers and sisters were of school age. In the end my grandmother did a deal with her eldest daughter. She would only have to stick with the family for two years while they got settled. After that she would be free to follow her heart wherever it took her. My mother gave in. Family always came first. (It must also be said that my grandmother disapproved of P. Mainly because of the age difference, but also because he was quite a possessive character and had an outspoken attitude to the church.)

P was distraught, so he decided to follow his love to England. And when he did, they planned to get married. But he couldn't get the travel papers he needed. My mother waited for years. To no avail. In the end, all they had to show for it were two piles of impassioned letters.

Before my mother and my aunt sailed for England with the rest of the family, they decided to have one last adventure in the east and do a tour of India. They left the family home in Rangoon in a horse-drawn gharry. P, realising that the love of his life was leaving, set off in hot pursuit, weaving through the rush-hour traffic. My grandmother, knowing that this was likely to happen, warned my aunt to make sure that my mother got on the plane that would fly them to Calcutta. My aunt was as good as her promise, and the two of them were on the plane by the time P reached the tarmac.

When they arrived in Calcutta a telegram was waiting.

    come back stop or wait there I'm coming to
    get you stop

Emotionally torn though she was, loyalty to her family prevailed over loyalty to her heart. There was also the fact that my aunt knew that she would catch hell from my grandmother if she didn't make good on her promise to deliver her sister safely to the rest of the family.

Naturally, my mother resented my grandmother's insistence on the family coming first. It didn't really help matters when my grandmother would say, 'One day you'll thank me for not letting you marry P.' Many years later, when P eventually did make it to London, long after my mother had met and married my father, she realised that my grandmother had been right all along. So, swallowing her pride, she did thank my grandmother. But obviously she didn't thank her anywhere near as much as me and my brother do.

P never married, but he did end up in England. I never met him. But for a long time he was a big part of my mother's life. And had things worked out differently he would have been my mother's husband. So who my mother is must, in part, be a result of who he was. And that's why, even though I never met him, I feel it right that I should thank him. That he was a fascinating man can, in my opinion, be gauged by the two other facts that I know about him. First, that he wrote a book that sought to resolve the whole science of physics into a single equation. Second, that he invented a new type of cat litter tray. So I imagine he would have made a quite singular father. But he would have been someone else's singular father.

This is probably a good point to clarify the sequence of events concerning my mother's itinerant family. My grandparents started the family in Burma. During the war they escaped to India and returned to their ancestral island home of Vypeen. Then, after the war was over, they went back to Burma to see if they could pick up the threads of their old life. As it turns out, they could pick up the threads. The only problem was that the threads were starting to fray at the edges.

The Burma they now found themselves in was not the Burma they had left. The country had gained independence and things were changing. My grandfather, though he got a job back working for the government, realised that as time went by he would probably become increasingly marginalised. What was of more concern, however, was the future of the children.

My grandfather was a firm believer in all things British. Prime among these was the British style of education, which his older children had already enjoyed. But now the schools were changing, and my grandparents were concerned about the education the younger children would get. Beyond schooling, the question of jobs and career prospects for them loomed large.

The family was, in effect, a group of immigrants associated with the old colonial structure in a country that had shaken off the shackles of Empire and was busy setting about promoting its own ethnically indigenous population. In retrospect, to my mind at least, this was obviously the right thing to do. For my grandparents and their young family, however, it was a turn of events that did not bode well for the future. So after six years back in Burma, the decision was made to pack their bags and start again somewhere new.

After considering various possibilities the obvious choice, especially for my grandfather, was Britain. So his eldest son was sent halfway round the world to check out the lie of the land. It must have been a most daunting journey. Particularly as the future of the whole family rested on what he reported back. He arrived at Tilbury docks on the twenty-fourth of July 1950. Within the first two weeks he lived at three different addresses and landed a job as a junior clerk with a firm of builders and contractors in Streatham, in the suburbs of South London.

Just under two years later the whole family arrived at Tilbury.

I asked my aunt what she remembered of the journey to England. She would have been seventeen at the time. She says that this boat trip, in contrast to the one on the *Chilka*, was very enjoyable. She remembers the food, the deck games and the onboard romances. But most of all she remembers when the boat docked in Naples. It's fixed so firmly in her mind because as she looked at the quayside and the swarm of activity there, she saw for the first time in her life a white man doing physical labour. If any one thing signalled to her that they were heading into a whole new world, it was this. A white man with a sack of flour on his shoulder.

When I asked her what she recalled of the food in Britain, her eyes lit up and she said that she remembered the fruit. And that the fruit was wonderful.

It was an answer that took me somewhat by surprise. After all, she had been born and had grown up in a world where fabulous fruit was piled high in the markets and sold for next to nothing. There were mangoes, papayas, pineapples, rambutans, mangosteens, custard apples, jackfruit, bananas big and small, yellow and red, guavas, oranges, Ugli fruit and much else besides. What did Britain have to offer in comparison? Apples, pears, plums, rhubarb, maybe strawberries in season. But as my aunt explained, it was these kinds of fruit that you couldn't get when she was small. All the while she'd been growing up she'd be reading about them in books or seeing them in movies. Occasionally, her father would return home from the market having tracked down a vastly expensive apple. This would be carried home like a trophy and the children would be summoned before the apple was carefully cut up into ten pieces. So the thought of coming to England and having, if you wished, a whole apple to yourself, was pure luxury.

I suppose the obvious lesson from all this is that what is 'exotic' is what is unusual. So a strawberry placed into the hands of someone who has been brought up eating mangoes becomes the height of intriguing, exotic sophistication. And, of course, vice versa. Which is how my mother's family must have appeared when they set up home in the frankly bland and unremarkable suburb of Norbury, South London, in 1952. Of course, the other reaction they probably encountered was the standard 'bloody foreigners!' one. But as Norbury is a typically English, restrained and anonymous neck of the woods, that kind of thing probably went on behind the buffering twitch of a starched white net curtain.

eight
P.S. BRING GROOM

My parents met in 1956. The encounter came about because my mother belonged to an organisation called the Legion of Mary. As its name suggests, it was something to do with the Roman Catholic Church. When my mother's family arrived in London from Burma and initially briefly set up home in a couple of rented flats in Kensington, finding the local church was one of the first things they did. The church would give them a grounding, and it would help introduce them to the new world they were in.

Life in Kensington was a shock to the system in so many ways. The family arrived with not much money, as the Burmese government at the time weren't keen on letting people take currency out of the country. One of the things they did manage to get out, however, was a large sack of rice. After all, when they turned up in England they would need something to eat, and among all the information my grandparents had managed to gather from their son's letters about the country that was to be their new home, there was nothing about the availability of rice.

The real hero of the move, and indeed of many of the years that followed, was my grandmother. She held the family together with an iron will and quietly ploughed through whatever difficulties they encountered. Somewhere in one of the notebooks in which she assiduously accounted for every single farthing that went out of the family budget, she wrote the following couplet:

> *I had a dream that Life was ... Beauty,*
> *I woke to find that Life was ... Duty.*

And if life was 'duty', it was a duty that she never shirked. In Burma she had been used to having servants to help her run the home. In London she took a job in a launderette at the end of the street, folding clothes for next to nothing, just to bring a bit more money into a household that needed every penny that it could get. After all, there were ten hungry mouths to be fed. And the host of noisy children would outgrow clothes at an alarming rate.

In the early days in Kensington, there was also the added problem of the family being split between two flats as they couldn't find a place big enough to take all of them. One of the ways my grandmother kept it all together was by cooking a big pot of curry every day. The problem was that the landlords were dead against allowing large numbers of people to gather together in their properties. So the family would have to wait until it was after dark before they could sneak into the flat where my grandmother had done the cooking and all gather for a much-needed family meal. And the food didn't just feed the body, it served the far more important task of nourishing the family as a family. When people eat together it builds bonds that strengthen with every mouthful. Of course, as you get older, you may want to escape those bonds, but the strength of the ties will always stay with you.

The church was another fixed point that helped the family find their feet. The Legion of Mary was an organisation that took the influence of the church out of the confines of the Sunday services and engaged the congregation in charitable and social activities. One of the first projects my mother was given when she went along to a Legion evening was to try to find out just how many overseas students there were in the area. This was because the church, realising that these incomers might often feel isolated and alone, wanted to offer the hand of friendship. It wanted to make the new people feel welcome. And, of course, it wanted to make sure that their spiritual needs were being catered for. But, to be honest, the prime motive wasn't evangelical. The prime motive was to make people from overseas feel welcome in a world that could all too often appear cold and hostile to newly arrived 'foreigners'.

So my mother and her sister would go round, knock on doors, ask a few questions, and invite anyone interested to the weekly afternoon dances that the Legion of Mary organised. One of the doors she knocked on was a flat at 59

Comeragh Road. One of the people she invited to a dance was my father.

Apparently, my father cut an intriguing figure. He was tall, dark skinned, neatly dressed, reserved but with a certain intensity about him. He was also very good-looking. Or so my mother thought – and who am I to disagree? At the dances he would hold himself just slightly apart from the bantering fray of excited young men and women. Hardly surprising then that it was his flatmate, my godfather, whom my mother first really got talking to. And through him she got to glean a few more nuggets of information about my father that only served to intrigue her more. For instance, the fact that he was a painter seemed very romantic.

When she did eventually get the chance to talk to him, the interest only grew. This despite the fact that for some reason he told her he was a Buddhist. It was for my mother, who came from such a staunchly Catholic background, a worrying development. The concern was only compounded when my godfather – a man who always liked a joke – chucked in the information that he wasn't sure if his friend was Buddhist or Muslim.

Despite this potential San Andreas fault lurking under the possibility of a relationship, my mother was most definitely interested in this man who seemed so at ease with himself, but quietly at odds with much of the world around him. As she got to know him, my mother began to realise just how provincial and deferential and hidebound by tradition her upbringing had been. In many ways, the values she had grown up with had all been about hierarchy and order. Her father had been, essentially, a government bureaucrat – and he not only worked for the system set up by the British in the east, but also believed in it. Allied to that was the importance of their faith and of the highly structured Roman Catholic Church in their lives. On top of all this you can add in the eastern tradition of the centrality of family.

My father, due to the experiences he'd had as he grew up, didn't believe in any of these things. Having said that, he did admire certain strengths and securities that he could see in my mother's tight-knit family, but he was also well aware of the stifling constraints that family life could bring.

Even though this was only fifty years ago, it was, in terms of how relationships developed, a different age. It was still a time when the word 'courting' could be used without a hint of irony. For instance, in all the time that my father and mother were seeing each other, they never went out on a date together. Of course, this isn't just because they lived in a different time to our own, but also because their ideas of how things worked were a product of a different world. In the east, things were even more formal than in 1950s London.

On the island of Vypeen, where my mother lived during the war, any potential relationship was not just about the two people involved, but about the two families. If you asked for someone's hand in marriage, the tradition was that you had to produce a near-calligraphed 'proposal' handwritten on something like parchment and formally present it to the family of your intended. Then, if the proposal was being seriously entertained, the elders of the proposer's family would get together with the elders of the other family and sing the praises of the apprentice groom. Then both sides would get down to the serious business of discussing the pros and cons of the potential union. As every family knew every other family it was very easy to get into the nitty-gritty of the imagined strengths and weaknesses of what might lie ahead. Then, if both families were happy, things could move forward. The vast majority of marriages were driven by love, but contrary to what the Beatles were to claim in the still unimaginable Swinging Sixties, love was not 'all you need'. It was far more complicated than that.

Given this kind of context, my father's courtship of my mother presented some very real difficulties for my mum's parents. Essentially, the big problem was that no one knew him. And no one knew his family. On top of that he might be a Buddhist. Or even a Muslim. And, as my grandfather reasoned, if he was a Muslim he could already have two other wives back in Ceylon.

Most of the time that the two of them spent alone together was perched on a sofa in the sitting room that was 'kept for best'. Even then they weren't really alone as it was a very small house, in which ten people lived, and the door to the sitting room was always kept open. In addition, there was the fact that my mum's younger brothers and sisters would often station themselves in the flowerbeds in the front garden and gigglingly peek in through the windows to keep an eye on what was going on. (My mother thinks that 'someone' may well have secretly 'suggested' that they do this, but she has no proof.)

But perhaps the real breakthrough in the developing relationship had happened a little earlier on a coach tour of Europe organised by Harry, a priest from Holland. Harry, who would go on to become a part of the family, was working with Indonesian students in Holland. The trip was primarily meant for these students, but to internationalise it still further invitations were also extended to churches in London. My mother and father were lucky enough to secure places. And though my father was at first pretty much as aloof as he always was, my mother engineered it so that she ended up sitting next to him on the coach for long stretches of the journey. As she coaxed him out of his shell, she discovered that he was widely read and could talk with both knowledge and insight about art, philosophy and religion. Maybe it was then that she decided that he was the man for her.

The wedding was set for the sixteenth of February 1957. But to get to that point certain obstacles had to be cleared. First, my father proved to my mother that he had, in fact, been baptised a Catholic, by showing her his baptismal record. (How he came to be a Catholic I have no idea. Especially as the aunt who raised him was a devout Anglican.) Then he applied for a non-impedimenta certificate from his parish priest in Ceylon that stated that he wasn't already married. Finally, he wrote a letter to my mum's parents formally requesting their approval of, and blessing for, the marriage. The letter, a crossed-out and amended draft of which I have in front of me now, ends:

I am writing to you realising the gravity of the request and being fully prepared to give of my best to make our life full of meaning and purpose, not forgetting the aim of creation.

My mother, not wanting to be left out, also ended up writing a letter. It was to her future brother-in-law in Ceylon. And its tone was somewhat different.

Now, how does one introduce oneself to one's future brother-in-law? Does one start from the bottom, grovelling in the dust, at the roots of one's family tree, or does one just blandly assume that one's forefathers are of no importance – 'What the man is now, is what counts,' so says Confucius. Well, I will leave 'one' to solve one's little problems whilst I continue. To help you form a glowing picture of what will be your brother's wife, I make a rapid mental assessment of debits and credits and try to be as impartial as possible, whilst I record, for your information, the latest statistics:

Name: Beulah Margaret Rebello

Age: Immaterial – OK, let's be frank – 22 (plus 4)

Nationality: Hard to say – tribe last heard of wandering aimlessly across plains of Mongolia in search of water for cattle. This particular specimen happened to be born in Burma.

Hair: Black

Eyes: Black (disturbing tendency to become slightly

crossed when violently agitated by declarations of love, thereby completely cooling the ardour of would-be wooers)

Appetite: Enormous
Height: 5 feet 4 inches
Weight: 8 stones
Waist: 24 inches
Feet: Size 5

(NB. These figures, however, are variable, dependent on weather conditions, conditions of the treatment by present proprietors, etc. – e.g. if immersed in boiling water, tendency to shrinkage, but if subjected to intense cold, heavy swelling around the waist will be discovered, accompanied by increase in weight due to abnormal intake of potatoes to combat the cold.)

And I bet you thought Bridget Jones was a totally original 1990s take on life.

The wedding dress was borrowed from a cousin. The cake was made by the mother of a friend. And the car that drove my mum to the church was lent by another acquaintance. After the service there was to be a small 'reception' back at the house. My mother remembers that the whole affair cost forty-seven pounds.

In a little red tuppeny notebook, my mother wrote a list of ten items that the best man had to take care of if the day was to go without a hitch. Item Four was a 'nip of brandy to fortify the bridegroom'. Item Five was a 'pair of handcuffs & piece of rope in case "he" tries last-minute dash for freedom'. And at the end of the list she has written a PS in capital letters:

P.S. BRING GROOM

Despite this instruction, my mum says that she was still not 100 per cent sure if my father would get to the church on time or, indeed, at all. So fifteen minutes before she was supposed to set off for her wedding, she insisted that one of her younger brothers cycle round to the church and make sure that the prospective groom was there. Only when the brother returned with the news that all was well did she come down the stairs of the family home and get into the waiting car.

Even though it was February, the day had dawned bright and clear. But it was very cold. My mother remembers kneeling next to my father on the two small stools in the central aisle of the church and shivering as the priest conducted the service. She shook so much that as fixed in her mind as the vows she was taking was the sound of her wooden stool rattling against the floor.

After the service the wedding party headed back to the family home where Technicolor photographs were taken in the back garden and where party food that spanned two continents was served. There were cocktail sausages, cheese cubes on sticks, assorted small cakes, and rice and chicken curry. But my mother was too excited to eat. And my father, after laughing and joking and accepting everyone's congratulations, stood in the back garden and smoked a Senior Service cigarette.

As the day drew to a close and the guests started to drift off, my mother went up to her room for the last time and changed into a going-away outfit. The truth was they were only going as far as my father's flat, as their honeymoon wasn't going to start until the next day. Then they would travel to stay in a cottage overlooking the sea on Caldey Island, off the Pembrokeshire coast of Wales. My mother and father said their farewells to the family, and then walked down to the bus stop at the end of the street to catch the first of the two buses that would take them to the flat. As they waited, one of the guests from the wedding drove past and, not quite believing what he was seeing, stopped to offer them a lift. Laughing, and grateful, the newlyweds accepted.

When they both got back to the flat, they realised that in the excitement and nervousness of the day neither of them had either wanted or been able to eat anything. Now they were ravenous. The only problem was that there was no food in the flat. So they went out for the rare treat of dinner in a restaurant. An Indian restaurant. My mother had chicken curry. My father had beef curry.

It seems a most appropriate way for my parents to celebrate the start of their married life.

* * *

To be an immigrant you need two countries. There's where you've come from. And there's where you go to. Both places have a past. Both places have a future. But you, as an immigrant, are caught somewhere in the present. You are affected by what's gone before. And you will affect what is to come.

My parents' histories as immigrants are one part of the story of how I ended up in aisle seven of Sainsbury's buying a jar of korma sauce. But there is also the story of how the jar got to be there.

eight
and a half

A BRIEF HISTORY OF CURRY
IN BRITAIN: PART ONE

To write a history of curry in Britain, you have to start with a history of spices. Start with a history of spices and it could easily be argued that what you're actually grappling with is a history of much of the world. That's because spices, and the pursuit of spices, have long shaped global trade, and played a major role in the rise and fall of empires.

As long ago as 2900 BC the ancient Egyptians were trading in spices. We know this because along with the other treasures found in their tombs, spices not indigenous to Egypt have been discovered. There also exist accounts of commerce with a land called Punt, which extended from the east coast of Africa to India. Physical evidence of the trade is recorded on the funerary monument of Queen

Hatshepsut – the only woman ever to declare herself Pharaoh – who died in 1482 BC. The reliefs show boats sailing to Punt to stock up on frankincense, myrrh and other spices. That the trade in ancient times through the Gulf was one with lucrative rewards can be gauged by the fact that numerous attempts were made to construct a canal across the Suez. Finally Darius I, the King of Persia, got the job done in about 500 BC.

The ancient Greeks didn't use a lot of spices. They mainly flavoured their cooking with the herbs of the Mediterranean. Cinnamon and saffron were the rare exceptions. And cinnamon is a most interesting example of how globalised the trade was even way back then. Originally, the only place in the world that cinnamon came from was Ceylon. So as early as 1500 BC the country was the start of a trade route. But a thousand years later, when the Greek historian Herodotus was writing, he assumed it was a spice from Arabia.

By the time the Romans rose to prominence and captured Egypt, the trade between the Middle East and India had been thriving for close on 3,000 years.

Rome got so enamoured of spices that at one point the emperor banned the use of gold to pay the merchants for them, as too much of the metal was heading out east and disappearing from the empire. Or, as the poet Persius had it:

> *The greedy merchants led by lucre, run*
> *To the parch'd Indies, and the rising sun;*
> *From thence hot pepper, and rich drugs they bear,*
> *Bart'ring for Spices, their Italian ware.*

Indeed, spices were such a symbol of status and wealth that at the funeral of his once mistress and then wife, Poppea, Nero ordered that all the cinnamon imported from Ceylon over one year be burnt as a sign of his grief. Mind you, Poppea was the woman who talked Nero into murdering his mother, his former wife, the philosopher Seneca, and may have first come up with the notion that Christians and lions were an amusing combination – so maybe Nero was having a bit of a knees-up to celebrate her passing. Then again, maybe 'knees-up' isn't the most appropriate turn of phrase, as one account suggests that Nero kicked Poppea in the stomach after she complained that he was spending too much time at the games and then watched as she bled to death.

In the world of spices, pepper ruled supreme. Its value was such that it could often be used as a form of currency. In France, at one point, a serf could buy his freedom with a pound of pepper. In England pepper was used to pay rent. But then, England being England, inflation kicked in and a 'peppercorn rent' ended up being a derisory amount.

Pepper was king for many reasons and not all of them culinary. Some professed that it was a cure for the poisonous sting of insects, others that when mixed with wine it could fend off colds, others still that it worked as a soothing ointment when pounded up in oil. But its primary claims to fame were related to eating. It was in demand because it could both disguise the flavour of 'ripe' meat and, more importantly, make salted meat palatable. That's why salt and pepper are a culinary combination that over the centuries has become hardwired into our collective taste buds. The Germans were so enamoured of the spice that, having sacked Rome, they demanded 3,000 pounds of pepper as a ransom. The next time you come across those German salamis coated in pepper, remember that what you are actually being confronted with is the medieval German equivalent of bling, as in, 'I'm so loaded I can afford to coat my sausages in pepper!'

What this love of the little black seeds meant in terms of world trade is pretty easy to understand, as originally pepper was only thought to come from the Malabar coast of India. So if pepper was to reach Europe, it would have to make the journey on long hazardous trips by both land and by sea. En route it would pass through the hands of many traders. At each stage of the journey, each dealer would add to the price their own mark-up. No wonder, then, that by the time it reached the dining tables of western Europe, only the wealthy could afford it in any real quantity.

The medieval times, the so-called Dark Ages, were when many of the most striking myths about the nature of spices grew and blossomed. As the knowledge was lost of where the spices actually came from, so legends took hold of the popular imagination. And they were legends that the medieval traders actively encouraged in an act of hype of which even a modern-day PR company would be proud. After all, the more mystical and magical the product seemed to be, the higher the price they could charge for it. (Just ask Laboratoire Garnier.)

One of the legends linked spices to rare gemstones, with both having been carried by river out of the Garden of

Eden into the world after Adam had eaten the apple and been chucked out of Paradise with Eve. (I know this casts God as little more than a grumpy park keeper, but you get the idea.) The Garden of Eden, the source of the spices, was rumoured to lie somewhere in the east. All of which added to the allure of spices, as not only were they prized for their curative and culinary powers, but also because they had come from Paradise itself.

Often the legends became very specific. Cinnamon, for example, was rumoured to come from the nests of certain birds. This was later refined to suggest that the only bird's nest it came from was that of the legendary, fire-dwelling phoenix.

And as human nature doesn't really change that much, there soon appeared in the sales literature for spices the one angle guaranteed to send the medieval share price of 'Spices 'R' Us' through the roof. Sex. Spices were said to be aphrodisiacs. Ker-Ching! In fact, Ker-Ching! Ker-Ching! Ker-Ching! It was, I suppose, what you'd call today the Viagra effect. What's odd is that even in modern times the legend lingers on. There is undoubtedly something sexy about spicy food.

However, back in medieval times the purported aphrodisiac nature of spices was probably only the concern of the rich. For the man on the top of the Clapham omnicart, his interest in spices was likely to be purely to do with livening up what was often fairly unpalatable fare.

Take Portugal, for example. Up to the 1400s it was not a wealthy country. Lives for the many were short and harsh.

Wars (predominantly with Castile) and disease were a constant threat. The Black Death had ravaged the country, leaving in its wake fields fallen fallow and religious extremism rampant in every pulpit. With not enough food produced even for its falling population, grain often had to be imported at treasury-draining expense. But if an ample supply of pepper could be secured, then meat could be preserved in winter, reliance on grain would not be so great, and a healthier and, indeed, larger population could be supported. On top of that, pepper could be sold to other nations and the coffers of the exchequer could start to bulge rather than empty.

Other factors that propelled the tiny nation of Portugal to the forefront of world exploration included an intense patriotism fuelled by endless wars against Castile and the Moors, religious fanaticism and the stoical nature of its people. Everything seemed to come together in the search for spices. The generations-long struggle to expel the Moors from their land was also a struggle against the Islamic faith. And people of Islamic faith were now the ones who controlled the flow of spices through the Middle East and into a Venice that had grown fat on the trade. So the search for an alternative route to the lands of the spices had a very strong religious imperative. It was not just about satisfying the needs of the body, or the desire for monetary enrichment, it was also about faith. It was, in many ways, a holy crusade to greater proclaim the glory of God. Indeed, it is often stated that when Vasco da Gama first landed on the west coast of India at Calicut, he ran ashore and proclaimed, 'For Christ and spices!'

Whatever his motives, the magnitude of Vasco's achievement can't be overestimated. He was the first European to sail all the way down the west coast of Africa, round the storm-lashed Cape of Good Hope, up the east coast, past Madagascar and Zanzibar, then across open ocean right the way to India. More importantly, he was also the first European to sail back. Unfortunately, by the time he got home he had less than one-third of the men he had set out with. Many of those who had survived were in a ruinous state of health from which they would never recover. Not that this bothered Manuel, the King of Portugal. Even before Vasco landed back on Portuguese soil, just word of his return alone prompted the king to add a globe to his royal sceptre and amend his title to:

> Dom Manuel, by the Grace of God King of Portugal, and of the Algarves on this side of and beyond the Sea, in Africa, Lord of Guinea and of the Conquest, the Navigation and Commerce of Ethiopia, Arabia, Persia and India.

He failed to add, 'And my dad's bigger than your dad, so ner!' but that was, I think, just because he didn't have any room left on the scroll.

What's surprising is that although Vasco had come back with cinnamon, cloves, nutmeg and pepper, as well as gems, it is commonly acknowledged that the actual amount of spices was little more than would fit in a bread bin. But spices were so valuable that even this paltry physical quantity is said to have been more than enough to cover the cost of the two-year expedition. More vital was the knowledge of the routes that he brought back. And in the years to come, pepper imports alone into Portugal rose to between 1,600 and 2,900 tons per year. The price that the pepper was eventually sold for was often thirty times what it had cost in India.

Little wonder then that the Portuguese crown, and more particularly Portuguese traders, grew rich and the nation ruled the seas. The big problem was that King Manuel spent all the money he got. Or, at very least, vast quantities of it. A problem that was compounded by the fact that he did nothing to organise and manage the trade in spices. As long as he got his cut, he didn't particularly seem to mind how things were run. As the country didn't have a large middle class, and having kicked out the Jews in a bout of religious fervour also lacked experienced bankers, the management and control of a burgeoning empire was a largely unsophisticated affair.

The Portuguese also expanded the lands under their flag far beyond what they could adequately control. Their settlements stretched from Brazil to the Azores, to west, south and east Africa, to the Gulf, to Goa and Cochin, to Malacca, to Java, and as far as Macau on the borders with China. With the bulk of the profits from the spice trade going to private merchants and not the crown, the chance of running such a far-flung empire in any coherent or even secure fashion disappeared.

Meanwhile, the Spanish had tried to discover an alternative route to India by sailing west. What Columbus actually discovered was America. In terms of spices, cooking and curry in particular, that's where things take quite a surprising turn. That's because in America Columbus discovered the chilli. He brought the plant, which he tried to pass off as a type of pepper, back to Europe, where it was unknown. What's more surprising is that it was also unknown in Asia. It was only after Columbus brought it back from America that the chilli made its way out east. Prior to that, the heat in, for example, Indian cookery would have come from pepper, mustard or ginger. So the one ingredient we probably most commonly associate with Indian food has only been kicking around on the subcontinent for little more than five hundred years. What's especially fortuitous for my story is that it is generally accepted that it was the Portuguese, having somehow pinched some chilli plants, or seeds, from the Spanish, who first carried the chilli to India.

Incidentally, this may also explain why my mother would often travel with a few chillies wrapped in a bag whenever we left the country to go on holiday. She said they were to add to the food we would encounter wherever we went. But obviously it was an unwitting homage to her Portuguese ancestors' great act of culinary largesse in first bringing the chilli to India.

The Portuguese and the Spanish dominated this newly booming spice trade for about the first hundred years. But by then the Portuguese had spread themselves too thin, and the Spanish had blown their lottery winnings on successive wars with the French and the British. All of which allowed the Dutch, who weren't preoccupied with fighting endless wars with their neighbours, to come up on the inside and snatch the top prizes.

By the end of the sixteenth century, the Dutch had gained control of the pepper trade. As a result the pepper price in London tripled. To try and break this Dutch monopoly, Queen Elizabeth the First granted a royal charter to a group of merchants on the thirty-first of December 1600. This was the birth of the East India Company. As its name implies, its main focus of attention was not originally India, but the East Indies, or, as it is now called, Indonesia. It was the place that had by then become the global powerhouse of spice production, thanks to its abundance of nutmeg, cloves and mace.

The first expedition of East India Company ships returned from Sumatra with one million pounds' worth of spices in the hold. On the way over it had stopped off in India, but only to trade cotton and linens before carrying on to the real destination. The problem was that the Dutch, who controlled much of Indonesia, didn't like the British muscling in on their territory. So they made trading there much more hazardous for the British. That's why the British switched their attentions to India, where the Dutch were also in control but not so focused on retaining power because the real prize for them were the spice islands of the East Indies – not India.

Some idea of how highly the Dutch valued the spice islands can be gauged by the fact that in 1667, when the Dutch had got the upper hand in the second Anglo-Dutch

War by breaking the chain in the Medway River, reaching Chatham and capturing the flagship *Royal Charles*, the terms of settlement they enforced on the British included the ceding of Surinam in South America to the Dutch and the handing over of the tiny island of Run in the Bandas Isles to them in exchange for their valuable American colony of Nieuw Amsterdam. To the Dutch it was worth it because the Bandas Isles were the only place in the world where nutmeg grew.

That Nieuw Amsterdam is now New York is something that the Dutch today probably don't mention that much in conversation. In many ways it has a weird feel of Jack and the Beanstalk about it. Except in this case the handful of beans turned out, in the long run, to be just that. And if they'd hung on to the cow, as it were, all of America could be speaking Dutch, not English. But at the time the Dutch were certain they'd gotten by far the better end of the deal.

In a similar fashion they probably thought that if they could hang on to the Dutch East Indies, what did it matter if the British took control of India?

nine
FISH

When I set out to tell this story, my mum gave me her mother's handwritten cookbook. It's a dilapidated and disintegrating affair on whose cover you can just about make out the printed words 'Student's Note Book' and 'Specially made for V.K. Kamath & Co, Princess Street, Cochin'. At the top of the cover, in words so faded they are almost impossible to read, my grandmother has written 'Knitting Patterns'.

Open the front cover of the book and pasted inside you find recipes cut from newspapers fifty years ago. The recipes are for Currant Dumplings, Golden Pudding, Lime Pickle, Snake Gourd Curry, Christmas Fry (Madras Recipe), Tomato Sambol and Pip, Squeak & Wilfred.

Pip, Squeak & Wilfred has absolutely no significance to any part of the story of my family. But it's got such a wonderful name that I just have to share the recipe with you.

PIP, SQUEAK & WILFRED

Put into a pan cold meat cut up into pieces, with
ready boiled peas, carrots, cauliflower, cabbage and
potatoes, with pepper and salt, and as much good
stock as will cover the meat and vegetables. Allow the
whole to simmer until the meat and vegetables have
absorbed half the stock, when it will be ready. Serve
very hot.

Next in the book is a sheet of paper, discoloured to a blotchy
oatmeal, with a pencil-traced outline of Britain on it. Who
drew it, why they drew it, and in which country they drew
it, I have no idea. And the thoughts they were thinking as
they outlined the boundaries of their future home are long
since gone to wherever hopes and dreams and fears go to
when we've stopped hoping and dreaming and being afraid.

A page on in the book, there is a poem inscribed about
the dangers of drink with the underlined title 'Wise Saying'.

Then the knitting patterns start. There's the Rose
Pattern, the Leaf Pattern, the Oval & Diamond Pattern and
on and on until forty-two crammed and handwritten pages
later you get the pattern for Bootkins II. (Not a patch, in
my mind, on Bootkins I, but then sequels never are.)

Only after that do the first handwritten recipes appear.
They are for Ripe Mango Chacha and Condensed Milk
Toffee.

As I leaf through the pages a whole new, but long-lost,
world opens up for me. If anything sums up the Anglo-
Indian life that my mother lived when she was young, it is

this fragile collection of papers that feels as ancient as an Egyptian papyrus unearthed from a sand-swamped tomb. A recipe for Salmon on Toast sits next to one for Dry Shrimp Ballichun. Instructions on how to make Imitation Lea & Perrins Sauce are followed by directions on how to make Pork Vindaloo. And then sandwiched between Easy Mango Pickle and Sa-Nwin-Ma-Kin (Burmese), you get the knitting pattern for a Child's Sweater.

Towards the back of the book is a page that gives the birthdays of my grandmother and grandfather, and all their children. I look down the list of names and find the aunts and uncles I grew up surrounded by. Each a distinct personality. Each with their own story to tell. Eight children whose lives would span the world.

Then among the eight names I see two more. Unfamiliar names. Names that now I can't help wondering about. Patricia Ramona. Born on the seventeenth of September 1937. Died on the second of June 1941. Genevive Bridget. Born on the sixth of July 1949. Died on the twenty-first of July 1951. Who were they? Who would they have been? What would they have given to the world?

In fainter writing is written, in brackets alongside the list, 'two miscarriages'.

Under the list of birthdays is a collection of twelve verses. There's this:

> *Let fate do her worst*
> *There are visions of joy*
> *Bright dreams of the past*

> *Which she cannot destroy*
> *Which come in the night-time*
> *Of sorrow and care*
> *And bring back the features*
> *That joy used to wear*

There's this:

> *Play up! Does it matter who wins or who loses?*
> *Play up, and play hard all the same*
> *There's plenty of bumps, and there's plenty of bruises*
> *They'll teach you much more than a game*
> *Take strength and good temper and courage and*
> * speed*
> *They're not a bad outfit for life and its need*

And finally, just to show that she always had the sparkle in her eye that I well remember even from her later years, when though the marbles might not have been permanently lost they were occasionally misplaced, there's this:

Girls
> *From birth to age 18 she needs good parents*
> *From 18 to 35 she needs good looks*
> *From 35 to 55 a woman needs personality*
> *And from 55 on, the old lady needs cash*

A page on from the rhymes there is a glossary of cooking ingredients translated from English to Burmese to

Hindustani. Then comes a handwritten recipe for Plum Pudding. Finally, holed up inside the back cover is a collection of loose pages carefully cut from various papers and magazines. From the *Rangoon Gazette* comes a recipe for Ceylon Curry (Another Way). From a 1951 magazine called *Home Notes* comes a collection of pancake recipes for Shrove Tuesday. And from a November 1952 copy of *Picture Post* comes an article that clearly illustrates just how different a world it was that my grandmother found herself in when she and her family ended up in England. The article is entitled 'All the World's Cooks in One Kitchen'. And this is how it starts:

> For two days cooking smells, ambrosial and appetising, filled the Festival Hall from cellar to roof garden and alerted the noses of passers-by 50 yards away. Nineteen nations, each with a team of three or four cooks, took part in the International Kitchen Exhibition organised by the Gas Council. The idea was to show just what succulent things can be done with the rations if you are willing to use recipes and assemble menus which, by 'meat and two veg' standards, are certainly foreign and, therefore, liable to be considered queer. All the raw materials used are available here, though some, notably those spices beyond the pale of 'a packet of mixed', need looking for in special neighbourhoods or shops willing to cater for the customer with outlandish ideas.

L.P. Hartley once wrote, 'The past is a foreign country: they do things differently there.' As I close my grandmother's cookbook, a cookbook that spans at least two different worlds, it's a phrase that comes back to me.

Now I realise that you'd probably like one of my grandmother's Asian recipes to try at home. Something authentic. Something you're not going to get in any other recipe book. And luckily I've found just the thing.

BRAIN WHITE CURRY

SERVES ?

1 brain
15 dry chillies, ground
1 pinch ground saffron
1 dessertspoon sliced red onions
2 cloves garlic
2 slices green ginger, chopped
2-inch-piece cinnamon
2-inch-piece rampe (leaf of the paudanus tree)
¼ stem lemongrass
small sprig curry leaves
¼ teaspoon fenugreek
1½ teacups coconut milk
salt, to taste
juice ½ lime

Wash the brain well in salted water and remove any skin or stringy pieces. Cut the brain into thick slices or cook it whole. Put into a chatty, add all the ingredients,

except the lime juice, and boil until the brain is cooked,
adding the lime juice when the curry is half cooked.

Do let me know how you get on with it.

A word of warning. All recipes are approximations. They
always are. Written down on a page in a cookbook, with a
glossy picture to illustrate it, any recipe gives the impression
that it's gospel. But it's not. That's why sometimes when
you try things out and you follow the instructions to the
letter, you still end up with a plateful of gloop that bears
only a passing resemblance to what the picture shows. And
when you come to taste it, you have the sinking realisation
that while you can't be 100 per cent sure what it should
taste like, you're 110 per cent sure that this isn't it. The
problem is that cooking is an art. So instructions implying
that if you carefully follow steps one through to twelve
you'll end up with precisely what you set off to make are a
lie. Such a twelve-step programme might work when you're
building a Froomby from Ikea, but it just doesn't wash
when you're making a Cloudberry ****ing Soufflé from
Gordon Ramsay's latest tome.

The problem is that while a recipe might list all the
ingredients you need, and appear to list all the things you're
supposed to do to them, it invariably misses out many
things that are equally important. In the case of Mr Ramsay,
for instance, recipes always miss out the following prepara-
tion-time details:

Live in Scotland: Become a professional footballer: Discover you're not going to make it: Turn your hand to cooking: Find out that you have a real talent for it: Work bloody hard for years in a succession of professional kitchens: Finally get your own restaurant: Work bloody hard in your own restaurant: Start to accumulate Michelin stars: Write your first cookbook: Get on TV: Discover you have a real talent for TV: Cultivate the foul-mouthed artiste persona that's pure meeja gold: Write more cookbooks: Do more TV shows (preferably that now are less about cooking and more about entertainment): Wake up to the realisation that you have now achieved the Holy Grail (or should that be Holy Gruel) of Cookendom and are no longer a person, but, queue fanfare of trumpets – A Brand. And a vastly profitable one at that.

Now assemble the ingredients to start cooking your soufflé.

If a recipe specified all the things you need to know to make a dish, it would be so long that you wouldn't buy the cookbook in the first place. And, let's be honest now, that's how we buy cookbooks, and indeed choose the recipes to cook from the cookbooks we possess. We leaf through the pages, get sweet-talked by a picture, then check out the recipe. Then we spot the long list of ingredients, and the longer list of instructions.

We think to ourselves: bloody hell, add 2 drops of boll weevil extract – I'm not going to buy a whole bottle of boll weevil extract just to use two drops of it and then have the rest of the bottle sitting around getting bored in the back of the cupboard for the rest of my marriage; definitely not doing that recipe.

Which is why we invariably plump for recipes that give the appearance of being only slightly more complicated than cheese on toast. Inevitably, we end up with something a tad disappointing. That's because all recipes are approximations. The instructions on my jar of korma sauce included as a caveat: 'All cooking appliances vary in performance, these are guidelines only.' But if we're really going full on for honesty here, it should also have said: 'All cooks vary in performance, these are guidelines only.'

And for Asian cooking it's more complicated still because every recipe that doesn't involve a jar should also carry this third, sobering disclaimer: 'All spices vary in performance, these are guidelines only.'

For instance, different chilli powders provide different levels of heat. But study chilli powders in their packets in a supermarket or down at the corner shop, and there is no way of knowing just how hot they are. You just have to suck it and see. (As it were.)

More confusingly, ground spices, once they are exposed to the oxidising effects of air, change. Over time they become less potent. So that half-used jar of garam masala that's been sitting in your spice rack for a year and a pinch is a subtly different kettle of fish from the one you originally bought.

Out in the east, things go off even quicker. So spices would be mixed and ground and blended on a daily basis.

Of course, it helped that over there a family didn't need to be particularly wealthy to have a maid or a cook to help with the preparation of food. For my mother the sights, the sounds and, above all else, the smells of spices being ground by hand with a venerable pestle and mortar are evocative of times and places long since gone.

Downstairs in my kitchen, shoved at the back of a cupboard that also contains a Moulinex food processor, a Braun hand-held blender and a George Foreman healthy-eating Baby George Grill, is my grandmother's old pestle and mortar. My grandmother's old, shamefully underused pestle and mortar. It weighs a ton. And appears to be made of something like granite. On rare occasions I do get it out. Within the crucible of its high-lipped bowl I crush cloves of garlic, various spices and peeled and diced nuggets of ginger. The weight of the pestle in my hand is strangely comforting. The solidness of the mortar that sits steady as I grind is somehow reassuring. And the very action of twisting and turning, with irresistible force into an immoveable object, feels like at last I am doing something real. I'm getting in touch with something I've lost. Or rediscovering something I didn't even have the sense to know I'd misplaced.

But I don't get the pestle and mortar out that often. Because it weighs a ton. Because it's shoved at the back of a cupboard and I'd have to get out the Moulinex, the Braun and the Baby George first. And then after I'd used it, I'd have to wash it up by hand or leave it to soak in the sink because I don't think I could put it in the dishwasher. But anyway the whole thing's academic because who's got time to grind spices by hand these days? And that's why my grandmother's beautiful pestle and mortar sits forlornly, gathering dust, at the back of a cupboard in the kitchen.

More fool me.

Back in the 1950s when my father was wooing (you remember wooing, it was real big at the time, happened in all the best movies, mainly to Doris Day) my mother, he was invited to her home and asked to cook a meal for her family. Unorthodox though my grandmother's method may have been, you must admit it was a cunning way of checking out a prospective son-in-law's suitability.

After all, what better test of a man's character and personality is there than the way he cooks? What's more, on an eminently practical level, if he were a good cook, at least my grandmother would know that her daughter would never go hungry. Even more practically still, if he proved to be a good cook, a welcoming host and able to get on with all my mother's cheeky and unruly siblings, then maybe the centre of gravity for a small proportion of family gatherings could be gradually shifted down the generational hierarchy. Which would give my grandmother a bit of a break.

My father probably just thought he was cooking them a curry. Little did he know that he was really up for an interview before a very hard-to-impress selection panel. Of one.

He made a meat curry. He used the spices that were at my grandmother's house. Spices he hadn't ever used before. Most critically of all, chilli powder that he had never used before. Half a century later, talk to my mother about that meal and she can still feel the burning heat of it scorching the roof of her mouth. She can still see the sweat beading and rivuleting down the forehead of her father. And she can still glimpse the somewhat forced wry smile of her soon-to-be-husband nonchalantly bluffing that this was how hot he had meant to make it all along.

When I recounted this story to my godfather in a snow-bound Boston, he burst out laughing. His interpretation of things cast the events in a different light.

When he and my father lived together in a flat, they would occasionally invite acquaintances and colleagues over for a meal. It was an act of typically Asian hospitality. The only problem was that they never had a lot of food to go round. Meat, especially, was expensive. But they would make a curry anyway. And if their guest was English, and especially if their guest was an English girl, they would, to quote my godfather, 'slam in the chilli powder'.

After just half a mouthful the hapless victim's head would explode with all the force of one of the wartime incendiary devices still, at the time, being discovered in bombsites all over the capital. Then the compatriots in crime would affect a pained and sympathetic expression and with heart-warming sincerity ask, 'Is it too hot for you, dear? Oh well, maybe you should just eat the rice.' And the still reeling and water-gulping guest would be struck by what a nice pair of kind young men these handsome fellows from Ceylon really were.

Once the guest had gone, the curry was consumed.

Whether the cooks were consumed with much guilt, I am in no real position to tell. Now whatever you think of the tactic, you've got to admire the ingenuity.

When we look back, do we see the world as it really was? Or do we remember what we choose to remember? Or do we remember what, try as we might, we can't forget? Looking back on my short-trousered days spent learning reading, writing and arithmetic at the Roman Catholic school at the top of our road, I distinctly remember having blancmange every day for pudding. I remember it because it was fluorescent pink, wobbled and had something of the texture of wallpaper paste about it when you eventually forced it into your cringing and whimpering mouth. I have no idea why they gave it to us because no one liked it. No one. Not even Dennis Murphy. And he ate everything. Even thinking about it now I start to feel a little bit sick. And this memory holds firm – that every day at St Anthony's Roman Catholic Primary School we were forced to eat pink blancmange – despite the somewhat contradictory fact that I can also remember the other puddings I ate at school.

A lot of the stories in this book come from my mum. They are stories she tells me now. Her memory is phenomenal. And her skill as a storyteller is far greater than mine. But the stories she tells are inevitably tempered by all the years that have passed since the events she recounts. But what did she think at the time? Unfortunately, of course, there is no way of knowing.

Well, that's what I thought. Then I came across this in a tattered envelope of old family photographs that she gave me. It is a short story she wrote. There is no date on it, only an address at the bottom that gives the details of the first house my parents lived in. It was the house where I was born. So, counting back, and because we moved out of the house when I was about four, the story is at least forty years old, which means that at the time she wrote it my mum had been living in England for roughly ten years. Who it was written for she can't remember. But that doesn't matter. Because, even though she couldn't have known it then, it was written for me, now, forty years on. And, of course, for you.

Fish

Normally of a naturally sunny disposition, my thoughts take a suicidal plunge each time I gaze into the depths of the yawning cavern of a fishmonger's stall in London.

On hygienically scrubbed white slabs, the bodies of those with common surnames lie buried together, collectively in a mound, ruthlessly stripped of the distinctive, endearing qualities they possessed in Life, tombstones haphazardly erected above each mound proclaiming callously to the peering inquisitive public – 'SKATE', 'HERRING', 'COD', 'PLAICE'.

Helpless bodies lie naked and staring, as if mutely beseeching: 'Have pity on a fellow creature in distress. Take me home with you. Wrap me up, at least in a coat of breadcrumbs, to hide my nakedness and to shake off the chill that I have developed from lying in state, embalmed in ice, in a common chamber, instead of being honourably laid to rest in the privacy of the family vault.'

On a short holiday in Italy, it filled my spirit with delight to see, once more, as in the east, everything in the fish shop alive and gesticulating wildly. The fish, prawns and crabs, kept alive in buckets and basins of water, joined vehemently in the brisk bargaining that was in progress, lashing their tails, wriggling, or waving their claws in the air – as if protesting at the low values for which they were being ransomed!

There was noise, dirt, confusion and a general welcoming stink of fresh fish, absent so long from the iced carcasses of fish displayed on marble-cold mortuary slabs at the fishmongers' all over London. In London, the fish, to my thinking, have absolutely no distinguishing taste or smell and I harbour the suspicion that the bodies have been scrupulously scrubbed with a detergent – 'Omo' or 'Daz' or some such appealing preparation – before being laid out lifeless, robbed of all personality, so that, to me, cod or skate, halibut or plaice all tasted alike, in spite of being labelled otherwise.

How absolutely frustrating it is, when one tries, with the skilful addition of various condiments, to inject some character into those sponge-like, tasteless carcasses, and fails miserably, merely succeeding in producing a gravy that is superb, whilst the fish lies remote – untouched (and untouchable) – supremely impervious, cold-bloodedly resenting all attempts to inject some endearing qualities into its flaccid flesh.

Fresh fish, straight from the nets, are the tastiest, of course. In the coastal areas in India and in Ceylon, fresh fish, crabs, prawns and oysters play the leading role in the daily menu. Come early morn', the fishermen melodiously call out their wares, their baskets, groaning with the weight of their catch, balancing expertly on their heads, bare toes digging deeply into the sand, as if coming to grips with Mother Nature herself. Toes – splayed out wide – unconventional and undeformed – free from the restrictive practices of civilisation, as uninhibited as the air, and the sea, and the elements around them.

Soon a brisk, merry bargaining session is in progress, with a great deal of banter and witty repartee exchanged between vendor and purchaser. If one lives close to the fishing nets, then the children, who eagerly watch the nets, come racing along, voices piping high with excitement: 'Come quickly and see the fish. The net's almost bursting wide open with its weight. Quick! Hurry!' One rushes to the water's edge to bid for the best catch. Or sometimes, at dusk, one sees a solitary, barefooted fisherman, riding home on his bicycle, alone and withdrawn, with only his pillion passenger for company – a giant fish lashed to his back seat.

One hears of restaurants, in Hong Kong and in Singapore, complete with little pools, where one takes one's monocle out to disdainfully scrutinise the passing swimmers, and suddenly, with a bloodthirsty jab of a fork, one pinpoints the fattest, laziest lobster and haughtily instructs the hovering waiter, 'Quick. Follow that fellow. I want him for my dinner.' The waiter expertly swoops down with a net, and the innocent victim is hauled out, struggling and gasping for breath, to be borne in triumph to the chef who, with little shafts of delight seeping out of his eyes, chuckling to himself, throws it into a pot, and, muttering low incantations, proceeds to make of it a magic brew.

Ah! There are so many delightful ways of approaching these gentlemen – our underwater friends. But, alas! In London, my heart cries out in sympathy at the indignities to which they are subjected after death.

All the world over, Londoners are noted for their almost impenetrable reserve. Of what nationality, then, are the fish in London? And why are they so tasteless? Has some of this characteristic reserve unconsciously seeped into their very fibres, so that they, too, hold themselves aloof, disdainfully repelling any attempts at familiarity? Or will their icy reserve, as I have discovered of my neighbours and nodding acquaintances, gracefully thaw out with the passage of time? I wonder!

A glimpse into the world my mother found herself in. A glance back at the world she found herself torn from. All crystallised in a haddock on a slab. Ask her today and she still maintains that fish in this country has absolutely no taste. And who am I to contradict her? But I think she was missing the point. That's because back then (and maybe even now) to the average Briton, lack of flavour in a fish was not a bad thing, but a good thing. To the average Briton, a fish that tastes too fishy is somewhat fishy. And should be avoided. Hence the nation's love affair with cod. A fish that tastes of nothing. Which is why this denizen of the deep has to be filleted, battered, fried in oil, drowned in vinegar, dredged in salt and, all too often, Tarantinoed in ketchup before it gets eaten. Mind you, do all that and it does taste brilliant. Essentially because you can't taste the fish. Which is just as well because cod doesn't taste of anything.

But what does this say about Britain, a country which, even though its diet does so little to reveal this, is an island? Perhaps the problem with fish for many of the inhabitants of this sceptic isle is that it is smelly. On top of this you can add in the fact that fish comes from the sea. Even the most cursory glance at a map will reveal that the sea around Britain extends from the glorious and gallant White Cliffs of Dover all the way over to the slightly dubious shores of the Continent. But, unfortunately, there is as yet no Sangatte-style bogus asylum-seeker processing centre anywhere on the seabed. All of which means fish can move freely about wherever they like. Which means there is a very strong possibility that fish are foreign.

So there you have it. Fish are smelly, and may well be foreign. And being smelly and foreign has, until recently, never been the most popular combination of culinary attributes a food could boast in Britain.

When I read my mother's story it struck a chord. In a previous life, when I imagined myself as South London's answer to Roger McGough, I wrote a poem about fish. Here is a taste of it.

And then to come across the men in white coats
selling fish
frozen fish
And I think
how strange to wake out of a cryogenic state
not into an era of fish enlightenment
in which fin rot
and other fish diseases
are things of the past
in which the parasites that cling to your scales
gorging themselves on free fish suppers
can be painlessly removed
but to find yourself dismembered
floating in a sea hotter than hell
in chunks
in a new shoal
with onions
and potatoes
and other things.
To come to consciousness in a curry.

I include this fragment of the poem not for any still linger-ing hope that it possesses merit, but as a way of illustrating a hitherto undocumented Theory of Genetics. Namely, the passing on of the propensity to favour certain literary metaphors from one generation to the next. My mother wrote about fish as a metaphor for certain aspects of immi-grant life. I wrote about fish as a metaphor for different aspects of immigrant life. Of course, I added in (and have spared you) a dash or two of underplayed melancholy and a pinch of thinly disguised existential angst, but, hey, I was a teenager, and that kind of thing was compulsory.

The only fish my mother had any real time for was mackerel. For a start it looked, just a bit, like the fish she remembered from her childhood. Maybe it was something about its shape. Maybe it was something about the glint in its eye. Or maybe it was the fact that if you held a really fresh mackerel up to the sun and turned its body over in your hand you would occasionally get a flash of iridescent colour. Colour that had no real place in a still drab, grey and sensationally rationed post-war London. Or maybe it was just because, to her Asian-educated palate, mackerel actually tasted of something.

Which also explains why, on the whole, the British don't eat a lot of mackerel. It's too strong-tasting, too fishy, and there's something worryingly Continental about its sleek and oily looks. Frankly, there is about it just the hint of a sharply suited, smooth-talking Italian charmer with slicked-back hair and pointed shoes.

In fact, peruse the usual suspects on display down at a 1950s fishmonger's and there was no escaping the sneaking suspicion that under cover of dark mackerel was a bit of a spiv. Get it down a back alley and it would probably whip open its glittering shot-silk waistcoat and try to flog you the piscine equivalent of a dodgy watch or a pair of knocked-off nylons. Or it would slip you something far worse. Flavour. And once you got a taste for flavour, then where would you be? Well and truly up the culinary duff, that's where.

No, dear, you're a nice girl, from a good family, you stay away from mackerel, you stick to cod, you can't go wrong with cod, you know where you are with cod.

The upside of all this for my mum (and hence me and my family) was that mackerel was cheap. So, fish-wise, we ate a lot of mackerel curry. We also ate a lot of an even cheaper fish: the tinned variety. While the locals, in their wisdom, grilled tinned sardines on toast reminiscing about the good old days of the Blitz or took out a tin of salmon for Sunday tea with the best china and doilies on the table, my mum would grab a can of pilchards from the middle shelf of the shop on the corner and head off home to stick it in a curry.

Oh well, you can take the girl out of Asia, but you can't take Asia out of the girl. And though I can't remember us going short of anything, the fact that tinned fish curry was a regular part of my mum's culinary repertoire probably meant we weren't really rolling in it.

So here it is. My mum's recipe for tinned fish curry. A recipe you won't find in any other recipe book. A recipe that won't ever be illustrated by a mouth-watering photograph.

A recipe that is completely inauthentic because in all the years my mum ran down to the beach to watch as the nets were dragged from the sea, never once among the wriggling and glistening oceanic plunder did she spot a 14-oz tin of pilchards in tomato sauce.

But, in so many other ways, it is as authentic as it gets. Because it gloriously illustrates what immigrants anywhere in the world have to do when they find themselves surrounded by unfamiliar choices and strictly limited options. You take whatever you can get and you make it work. And maybe, if you work hard at your job, and your kids knuckle down and get a good education, somewhere, years down the line, you'll discover that tinned fish curry has become a thing of the past.

Then you'll find yourself down at the fishmonger's staring at everything that's on offer and realising that you can afford whatever you want. In the words of Del-Boy, 'The world is your lobster.' The only thing that is certain is that you'll never, ever, buy cod.

TINNED FISH CURRY
SERVES 3

1 x 425g tin pilchards in tomato sauce
1 medium onion, sliced
oil for frying
5 curry leaves
2 cloves garlic, sliced
2 slices ginger

½ teaspoon chilli powder, ½ teaspoon ground cumin,
     ½ teaspoon ground coriander, ½ teaspoon turmeric,
     all mixed together
salt and lemon juice, to taste

Fry the onions in a little oil, then add the curry leaves. When the onions are transparent, add the garlic, ginger and spice mix. Add a bit of water and wait for the oil to come to the surface. DON'T LET POWDER BURN – everything then tastes bitter. Add water if necessary. Add tinned fish and enough water to make gravy. Season with salt and lemon juice.

Optional: Add two dessertspoons of yogurt – this will give a sourer taste. Or lemon juice, vinegar or lemongrass for the same result. Or add a blob of coconut cream. This will give, unsurprisingly, a slight coconutty taste.

Incidentally, the house where my mum wrote the story about fish, the house where I was born, was 8 Fairview Road, Norbury, South London. It's not there any more. It got knocked down and redeveloped years ago. In its place they built a Sainsbury's.

I'm beginning to think that those bastards have got it in for me.

nine
and a half

A BRIEF HISTORY OF CURRY IN BRITAIN: PART TWO

In the early days of the European adventures in India, many nations set up ports along the coast. As India was made up of numerous separate states, each run by their own ruler, it was easy for each European incomer to find somewhere to pitch tent. All the more so as neighbouring rulers were often in the grip of generations-long conflicts. The infighting between the locals made it all the more tempting for the Europeans to try to seize overall control.

The French were particularly keen on kicking out their European rivals. They even funded an uprising against the British that was eventually crushed by the East India Company man Robert Clive. It was an event that marked the rise to dominance of the British in India.

The Portuguese, as well as suffering because of the lack of a coherent administrative structure and colonial possessions scattered too far and wide, also fell foul on another score. Ironically, what turned out to be their Achilles heel was one of the very things that led them to discover the route to India in the first place. The problem was that when they arrived, as well as the monsoon winds that filled the sails of their vessels, they were also powered by a desire to spread the word of God. When they landed in India they weren't just sailors and traders, they were missionaries too. And particularly zealous missionaries at that. Unfortunately for them, the local peoples they encountered had plenty of gods of their own and didn't really see the need for a new one.

The British, when they started arriving in numbers, were pretty much unconcerned with spreading religion. Obviously this went down far better with the locals. And whereas the Portuguese sailors were often already family men, and indeed sometimes brought their families with them, the British incomers tended to be single. So with the British there was more intermarriage and a lot more, let's just say, 'intermingling' with the Indians.

The other relevant factor about the British male is one that's only begun to change in the last twenty years. Namely, they couldn't cook. So they were soon succumbing to the temptations of the local cuisine. All of which casts the first large-scale encounter between the British and curry as something akin to a load of lads on the loose after a hard day's work, settling down somewhere to scoff something cheap, tasty and filling. Which, when you think about it, is exactly what happened over three hundred years later when the curry boom of the 1970s hit the high streets of Britain.

Reverend Edward Terry, the chaplain at the first English base set up at Surat in 1618, described one of the dishes he encountered like this: 'Among many of the dishes of this kind, I will take notice of one they call deu pario, made of venison cut in slices, to which they put onions and herbs, some roots with a little spice and butter: the most savoury meat I have ever tasted and do almost think it that very dish which Jacob made ready for his father, when he got the blessing.'

Over the following years the East India Company inveigled its way into the good books of one ruler after another. Soon they had become the prime commercial force in the land, taking a slice from almost every transaction. Unsurprisingly the company's profits boomed. So did the wealth of the people who worked for it. Young men flooded out from Britain hoping to accrue in a few years a financial stake that it might take a lifetime, or indeed generations, to build up in Britain. When the successful company men returned home they were so loaded, and so vulgarly nouveaux riches, that they got the backs up of too many people for their own good. I suppose much of the old money looked upon these cash-laden newcomers the same way as today's Home Counties set might look upon the sudden arrival in the local manor house of a bunch of extravagantly sun-tanned lottery-winning chavs.

So, in the best of British traditions, 'something had to be done'. And it was. In 1818 the British government started to take over control of the 360 Indian provinces that the East India Company ran. It was the somewhat induced birth of the British Empire in India. No longer would the continued conquest of the subcontinent be done in the name of a commercial company. It would be done in the name of Britain. But, of course, commerce would still remain the major driving force. India, though most of its people were poor, was rich in so many ways. And all those riches now came under British rule.

The first Viceroy of India was appointed in 1858. Between then and the start of the First World War in 1914, the British Raj enjoyed a long golden summer. Unfortunately for the majority of the people under the rule of the British in India, it wasn't really a summer that they could put their feet up and enjoy. Even the most cursory viewing of *Carry On Up The Khyber* would convince you of that.

Perhaps the most significant development in the history of the British Raj and its burgeoning love affair with Indian food actually took place in the Middle East. Ironically, it happened along the very spice routes whose monopoly was smashed when Vasco da Gama first sailed to India. In 1869 the Suez Canal was opened. As a result, the length of time it took to sail from England to India was halved. What this meant is that many more British women made the journey out and set up home on the subcontinent. The memsahib had arrived.

Previously, the men who ran India had been content to let their local cooks serve them local food, especially when they were off up country, pith-hattedly teaching the natives about cricket, railways and the need to pay taxes. But with the arrival of the memsahib things changed. Often in charge of households with twenty or more staff, they had plenty of time to instruct the cooks in how things were done back in England. In the cultural and culinary clash that ensued, Anglo-Indian cooking emerged. Roasts and game pies and high teas did battle with chicken kormas, chapattis and kofta curries. Mulligatawny became the soup of choice and soon fusion dishes like the (in my opinion) ridiculously overrated kedgeree became popular.

Incidentally, the word 'mulligatawny' comes from the joining together of two Tamil words – *molagu* and *tunni* – which mean pepper and water. The dish comes from the southern Indian province of Tamil Nadu. So this makes the British mulligatawny a distant relative of the rasam my father brewed up whenever he had a cold in London. But compared to the standard British soup, my father's version was the kind of distant relative that would turn up at a family wedding, drink all the booze, snog the bridesmaids and probably nick a couple of the presents too. It was a soup that took no prisoners, rather than an amusing reminder of the days of the Raj.

But all the while that the British were in India they were developing a taste for, and indeed love of, Indian food that was getting embedded deeper and deeper into the very fibres of their being. When they came back to Britain they started to long for a taste of the 'old country'. And the 'old country' for them had become India.

What is probably the earliest recipe for 'currey'

recorded in English came in 1747 in Hannah Glasse's *Art Of Cookery ... By A Lady*. Hannah's recipe, 'To make a Currey the India Way', combines 'two Fowls or Rabbits' with onions, butter, peppercorns and some browned coriander seeds. And sounds awful.

By 1773, the Norris Street Coffee House in Haymarket had curry on the menu. By 1780, the first commercial curry powders were on sale. Curry powder is, in most likelihood, a British invention. In India curries would be made with fresh spices, which the servants would grind into a masala on the day it was to be used. Back in Britain fresh spices were unavailable, as were the retinues of knowledgeable cooks and servants to grind them daily in the correct proportions. As a result, curry powders, which promised all the taste without the grind, were probably seen as the easiest way to get the 'authentic' flavours of India.

In 1784, Sorlie's, a perfumery in Piccadilly, plugged curry by saying that it 'renders the Stomach active in Digestion – the blood naturally free in Circulation – the mind vigorous – and contributes most of any food to an increase in the Human Race'.

Probably the first Indian restaurant of any note was opened in 1809, at 34 George Street, near Portman Square in London. It was called the Hindoostanee Coffee House and was the work of Sake Dean Mahomet. Mahomet had been orphaned in Patna in the 1760s and had started to work for the East India Company as an eleven-year-old in 1769. He ended up in the employ of Godfrey Baker, an Anglo-Irish officer. When Baker went back to Ireland,

Mahomet followed him. He stayed working for the Bakers, but ended up marrying an Irishwoman, Mary Daly, who may have had money. In 1807 he moved his family to London and two years later opened the Hindoostanee.

The Coffee House was decked out with bamboo furniture, Chinese pictures and other 'Asiatic embellishments'. All of which makes it sound very *Changing Rooms*, but for its day it was revolutionary. He advertised his food in *The Times* as being 'in the highest perfection and allowed by the great epicures to be unequalled to any curries ever made in England'. His target market was clearly defined as returning EIC officers. The restaurant did well at first but soon lost out to the Jerusalem Coffee House near the Cornhill Exchange, which mopped up the custom of merchants with trading links to the East India Company.

The Hindoostanee shut up shop in 1833, long after it had driven its original owner into bankruptcy in 1812. Not that Mahomet was down for long. He relocated to Brighton, opened a bathhouse and ended up as Official Shampooer to His Majesty George IV. He is also reputed to be the first Indian to have written a book in English. All of which makes him sound like a remarkable cross between Madhur Jaffrey and John Frieda.

But perhaps the most influential threat to these first Indian restaurants came from that great bastion of social life at the time – the club. The Oriental Club in Hanover Square served curries, as did its rival, the Reform. If returning India hands could get their curry fixes at their clubs, why should they go to an Indian restaurant outside? Also, domestic households were becoming exposed to Indian recipes in the cookbooks of the day. For example, Mrs Beeton's *Book of Household Management* eventually included fourteen curry recipes.

What's more, at the very pinnacle of society curry was soon finding favour. Queen Victoria was a curry lover. At her holiday pad of Osborne House on the Isle of Wight, she always liked to have a curry on the menu. Her fascination with everything to do with the subcontinent was only heightened when she was presented with two Indian servants on her Golden Jubilee in 1887. They were essentially gloriously liveried table staff, but she soon had them ensconced in a section of the kitchens grinding up fresh herbs and spices for daily cooking. Apparently, her favourite was rice, daal and chicken curry.

Victoria, despite being the Empress of India, never had the chance to make a trip to the subcontinent. Albert, her husband, did. And on his travels he is reputed to have stopped off at the Madras Curry Club just to sample their madras prawn curry. Back on board his ship the *Seraphis*, the French chef was given curry lessons by Indian cooks. But when Albert tasted the results, he was not amused: 'The French intelligence, fine and keen as it is, does not penetrate the depths of curry lore, and the dishes, even after considerable experience in the arts and sciences of several gentlemen of colour engaged expressly to dress curries, never came up to the Indian standard.'

It is, you must agree, a most revealing statement as to the esteem in which curry was held in the highest of circles back in Victorian times. But what I find most striking about Prince Albert's words is that well over a hundred years ago he both understood and was expressing a theme which has only recently come to the fore in contemporary culinary circles in Britain. Namely, that the cooking of a curry could be as complex and sophisticated as that of the highest of French haute cuisine.

The most famous Indian restaurant in Britain was opened by Edward Palmer in 1927. Palmer is interesting for many reasons, and although he was undoubtedly an English gentleman, he did also have an Anglo-Indian strand in his genetic make-up. One of his great-grandmothers was Begum Faiz Bux, a Mughal princess, who had become the wife of Lieutenant-General William Palmer, an English officer serving in India. During the British Empire Exhibition of 1924, Palmer ran a restaurant called the Mughal Palace, catering for the hordes of visitors who descended on Wembley where the show was held. Such was his success that he decided to replicate the cooking in a permanent restaurant in the West End.

The restaurant was called Veeraswamy's and the site he settled on was at the Piccadilly Circus end of Regent Street. The decor echoed an East India Company clubhouse from the height of the Raj. And the food drew rave reviews right from the start. The menu included at least twelve different curries, such as madras chicken curry, mutton and lentil curry, prawn curry and a selection of vegetable curries, as well as birianis, kebabs and even an Indian omelette. And to make sure that the less adventurous eater was catered for, there was also English rump steak. (But there's no mention of chips, or, for that matter, tomato ketchup.)

Veeraswamy's soon became the haunt of the fashionable and the famous. Prince Edward was a patron, as were the kings of Denmark and Sweden, and Charlie Chaplin. Though, obviously, they didn't all turn up on the same night.

While Veeraswamy's catered for the rich, further down the food chain (as it were) Indian cooking was also starting to put in an appearance. Initially, places serving curries would be found mainly near the docks in East London. These cafés would cater for the Lascars – Indian sailors – who found themselves in London hankering after a taste of home. These sailors would often come from Sylhet, a land-locked region which is now part of Bangladesh. Though Sylhet has no coast, it does have rivers and these were navigated by steam ships that local workers learnt how to run. Their knowledge would take them to Calcutta, where they would often be hired on ocean-going ships that carried them around the world. (Incidentally, the shipping companies loved them because they could be paid considerably less than sailors from Europe.)

The small cafés acted as more than just places to eat, and soon became unofficial meetinghouses and community centres. So much so that when the British government got worried about the rise of Indian nationalism, they despatched agents to keep an eye on what was going on while the endless plates of rice and curry were being dished up and devoured.

From being canteens and meetinghouses and community centres, it was a small step for the restaurants to become job centres too. For the Indian sailors with no jobs in London, finding employment was always going to be a struggle. Hardly anyone would give them work. One notable exception were the Bahadur brothers, originally from Delhi, who had come to England to study, but had opened Indian restaurants instead. By 1945 they had premises in London, Brighton, Oxford, Cambridge, Northampton and Manchester. Almost all their staff were ex-seamen from what is now Bangladesh.

And I would argue that, rather than in the likes of places like Veeraswamy's, it is within this group of people that the real roots of Britain's curry boom lie.

ten

A SWIRL OF BLACK

I don't know how to break this to you, but most of you are eating curry all wrong. You go to a restaurant, order what you fancy, wait for it to be cooked, then eat it. Or you get out a recipe book at home, buy the ingredients you need, cook the food, then eat it. Or you go to a friend's house, where they've done the buying and the cooking, and then you eat what is offered.

All of which sounds very reasonable. And maybe I'm overstating things a bit by saying you're eating curry all wrong. But the point I'm waltzing around is that to be truly honoured by your host, the really prized invitation is not one to come and eat on the day the food is cooked, but on the next day. That's because, as my father's sister frequently pointed out, curry tastes better on the day after it is cooked. Her theory was that on the day of cooking itself, the various spices taste as if they are competing

171

with each other to draw attention to their own particular flavour.

She went on to reason that the day after you cook a curry the spices have not lost their identity, but instead harmonise more with other spices in the dish. This is particularly true for chillies, which early on in a curry's life cycle tend to throw their weight around, yobbishly bellowing their hardness like a lagered-up England fan, intimidating all the less aggressive flavours. The day after cooking, the lager has worn off, the fan has calmed down and, while still being an England supporter, has no desire to scare the locals with his tattoos.

The consequence of all this, when I was growing up, was that whenever my parents cooked for a big party, while the food on the day was wonderful, the day after it was even better. No doubt it was also better because on the day afterwards the pressure was off. So my parents could relax and eat and not worry that the guests were all right and had 'enough to eat'. But mainly the food was better the day after because it was better. The spices were less angular, the flavours more rounded, the meat more infused with the tastes of the gravy that surrounded it.

By contrast, in the west there is no real tradition of food tasting better the day after it is cooked. Roast a joint of beef, and while sandwiches made from it the following day can be mighty fine, the beef itself is at its best half an hour after it has come out of the oven. Go to a fancy restaurant, or better still watch any of the TV shows that take you inside the kitchen of one of those establishments, and the whole frantic, tension-filled, testosterone-charged performance is about getting food on the diner's plate at a peak of perfection.

Maybe what I'm getting at is a philosophical point. In the west, with food, it is all about the moment. One particular moment. And you're either working up to that moment or coming down from it. In the east, in general, and in particular with a curry, it's not about a moment, it is about an ongoing state. Cook a curry for dinner guests and it doesn't matter if they turn up half an hour late. In fact, follow my logic, and it's probably better if they turn up not half an hour late, but half a day late. That way the curry will be even tastier.

What's more, this analysis of how food works in the two different cultures could equally well be applied to attitudes to life itself. Maybe in the west life is often viewed as a soufflé, but in the east people know it's really a curry.

Which brings me to the subject of leftovers.

Leftovers, in the west, are things that have been, surprise, surprise, left over. They are what has not been eaten, but has not yet been thrown away. And they have a certain stigma attached to them. To eat leftovers is somewhat of a chore. You eat them because you have to. Because you don't want to waste food. Because you can't be arsed to cook something fresh. But if a curry tastes better the day after it is cooked, then where does that leave the leftovers? In my opinion it leaves them as something not to be shunned, but to be celebrated. Go round to someone's house and be told that you're going to be eating leftovers, and you are a very lucky person.

The irony is that should you peruse the likes of a 1970s *Woman's Own*, for instance, the chances are that if you came across a feature on cooking a curry it would inevitably inform you that a 'curry' was a very good way of using up 'leftovers'. While this may well be true, I hope that you can see by now that this would be completely missing the point.

Personally I blame Coronation Chicken. A dish invented by Constance Spry from Le Cordon Bleu School in London and served at the Queen's coronation lunch in 1953. It was a dish that plonked already cooked chicken in a mild curry sauce that was about as exotic as something really, really unexotic. Luckily for all of us, its popularity has gone much the same way as that of the Royal family itself. Having said that, I have heard rumours that the latest delight to be added to Prince Charles's Duchy Originals range of foods is a packet of cook-in sauce – whose recipe the prince himself created – called Abdication Chicken. But this might just be a rumour.

The other way that you're probably doing the curry thing all wrong is that when you do cook for your friends, you cook the quantities the recipe gives you. So if there are going to be four of you for dinner, you cook enough curry for four people.

While this may be logical, to the way I was brought up it is anathema. In my home, whenever a curry was cooked, you always made too much. This was a legacy of the far more socially relaxed and interactive worlds that both my mother and father grew up in. In Ceylon, and India and Burma, you never knew who would be drifting by at a mealtime. If someone did stick their head through the door, the only hospitable thing to do would be to ask them to join you for lunch, or dinner (or even breakfast).

Also, cook more than you need and you can save what has not been eaten for the day after. When the flavour of the feast will have improved with age. These days you can stick what's left in the fridge or the freezer. And should someone turn up unexpectedly all you have to do is cook some rice and get out the leftovers, and you can strengthen your friendship over something far more satisfying than a sandwich.

Another point is that you're not only cooking far too little curry, you're eating far too much of it. A contradiction, I know, but let me explain what I'm going on about. The problem arises because in the west when people eat rice and curry they tend to eat too much curry with not enough rice. In the parts of India where rice grew it was the staple, it was the food that, primarily, sustained the mass of the population, and a curry was the addition that supplied the flavour. Moreover, the curry was usually just one of several contrasting and complementary dishes that served to provide a balanced meal. But the key thing here is that these other dishes were served in small quantities. You had your rice, then a little of this, a little of that, and by carefully combining what was on offer, you ended up with a delicious meal. Hence in a curry, large quantities of meat or fish were never really necessary.

In this way, a curry could be seen working as a 'rice-puller'. I'm not sure of the precise definition of the term, but the gist of it seems to be that it was something that gave the bland rice an intense shot of flavour to elevate it far beyond just palatable into something mouth-watering. Rice-pullers were often sambols, or pickles, or, I would argue, curries.

But when the east met the west, whether it was back in the days of the Raj or in the East End restaurants of the 1960s, the western male appetite expected a certain quantity of meat or fish in order to feel well fed. The result is that all too often in an Indian restaurant when you order, for instance, a roghan josh and a portion of rice, both come to the table in dishes that are the same size. And that's where it goes wrong. That much curry should never be eaten with that little rice. Hardly surprising then that in the 1960s and 1970s Indian food soon acquired the reputation of being delicious, but also of giving you ample time to sit down and 'read the newspaper'.

If you want a better idea of the proportions in which curries should be eaten, go to a restaurant and order a thali. Then you'll get a silver tray covered with a selection of foods in little dishes. What curry you get will be served in a portion that at first sight might seem small, but is far more authentic, and far better for you. But, in my opinion, they still won't give you enough rice. Then again, I am quite greedy.

Of course, all these instructions telling you that the way you're eating curries is wrong, while being on one level true, are on another level cobblers. I have no right to tell you how to eat. You should do what you enjoy doing. I suppose I'm just pointing out that there is another way of going about things.

* * *

When you're young, what you grow up with seems normal. You think that everyone lives the same way. So I grew up thinking that after all my primary school friends went home, they too sat down to rice and curry for dinner. It was only after I started going to friends' houses to play that I made the somewhat shocking discovery that after a day in which the school dinner ladies served up sausage and mash, or fish and chips, or meat pie and potatoes, my friends would go home to eat the same thing all over again. While it was a revelation, it wasn't necessarily a disappointing one. That's because the food at my friends' houses was much better than the food at school. Not that the cooks at school were bad, and indeed compared to what Jamie Oliver has revealed about school cooks today they were veritable Michelin-starred chefs, it's just that school meals were mass catering. And it's hard not to have your sausages dry out if you have to cook three hundred and then keep them warm in the oven.

The other reason that the food at my friends' houses wasn't disappointing was that, for me at least, it was novel. English food after school was not something I was used to. And even if I hadn't liked what I was offered, I would have eaten it anyway. That's because I was what was called at the time 'brought up properly'. Not to eat something that someone had cooked for you would have been rude. After all, you were a guest in their house. On top of that, I was greedy. So the chances of me leaving anything on my plate were always pretty slim. Unlike myself, of course.

At the time I didn't think much about being 'brought up properly'. Now that I've got children of my own, I'm finding the proposition an altogether different kettle of kippers. Most of the time I feel that I'm not succeeding in 'bringing them up properly' and I'm having my work cut out just to 'keep up with them'. As for mealtimes, I'm frequently confronted by the problem of getting them to eat. When I was young, the problem was more along the lines of getting me to stop eating. Odd. Very odd.

When I was growing up, I also thought that living in a house full of paintings was normal. I thought that everybody's father painted pictures. For as long as I can remember, there would be times when me and my brother couldn't disturb my father because he was up in the attic working on a painting. We did, occasionally, venture into the room, where our father, far from getting cross with us, would indulge our idle curiosity. But because it was just a normal part of everyday life, it wasn't that interesting.

In many ways, him painting was just as unremarkable as him doing the ironing. Caught up in the endless summer holiday of childhood, it never occurred to me to watch what he was doing closely. Or to ask him any questions about it. But if the choice is between sitting in the attic watching your father occasionally lifting a brush to a canvas, or legging it down to the park with your mates to build a fort out of dumped tyres or dam the stream with plundered wood to create a backlog of water deep enough to push each other into and get drenched from head to foot, it's not the room at the top of the house that gets the vote.

The paintings themselves are hard to describe. Maybe it's just that I don't know the right words, or have sufficient skill with the words I do know. When I look at one of the pictures now and try to translate what I see into words, I find myself floundering about aimlessly as if I was trying to tell you what the colour blue is like when you haven't ever seen anything blue before.

The earliest pictures, from the late 1950s, were stark and brutal black and white. The canvases, or more accurately, hardboard-backed paper since canvas was expensive, are covered in broad sweeps of swooping paint. Others have angular brushstrokes applied confidently but almost casually. Hardly any white space remains. Later the paintings became softer. More rounded. With swirling spherical themes recurring. From the stark black and white, the palette had evolved into one encompassing shades of grey. The texture of the paint application seems to be as important as the forms created.

Whereas the earlier paintings might have been the product of a mind trying to fix and record the angular coldness and the anonymity of the harsh new world he found himself in, the later works were more contemplative and spiritual, and seemed to imply that in order to understand the world around us we had to understand the world within us.

I do wish I'd asked him more about them at the time. But even if I had, I don't think he would have explained. Because pictures weren't meant to be explained. They were meant to be experienced. Only in that experience would any meaning, if there was to be a meaning, become apparent. I also believe that my father thought that any work of art was about communication. It was, in effect, an exchange. Half of the exchange was what the artist brought to the process of creating it. The other half was what the viewer, reader or listener brought to the process of viewing, reading or listening. And the third half is what is created when these other two halves come together. That's why when any work of art connects with you it always results in more than the sum of its parts. So a half plus a half equals one and a half. Or sometimes even seven.

I never considered how 'good' the pictures my father painted were. It was a question that never came up. And, I suppose, if it had come up I wouldn't have had any context in which to make a decision. Or, more accurately, any context I might have been able to develop would have been inevitably influenced by the facts that:

A. I grew up with the pictures.
B. My father did them.

Two of the pictures hang at the top of the stairs outside the door of the attic room in which I'm working. I am struck by the fact that I'm working in exactly the same way that my father did. Alone in an attic room, before the rest of the family wake up, listening to the birds in the street outside the window, lost in some other place, trying to fashion something coherent out of the materials to hand, hoping that whatever I come up with will somehow connect. The first of the two pictures dates from 1957. Five years before I was born. In it a swirl of black paint creates a vortex that pulls the viewer into a point somewhere far beyond the flat plane of the image. The second picture was done in 1983. A grey lozenge is contained within a thick U-shaped line of darker grey that curves over at the top, almost totally enclosing it. Within the lozenge there is a small black circle floating above a three-pronged star.

The first image is all turbulence. The second calm. Maybe that says something about the journey my father made in the twenty-six years that lie between the two pictures.

Ferreting through a box of papers to find out more about my father's work, I came across a programme for an early show of his from the 1950s. And I found some reviews. Reviews that were startlingly good. By the 1960s the shows had died out. The problem, I think, was that he was out of step with the times. His early work was, I believe, what was termed Abstract Expressionist. The 1960s moved away from such works as Pop Art exploded onto the scene. Pop Art seemed to be a movement in thrall to colour, and commercial references and surface. What my father did was nothing like that. It was more austere. More thoughtful. More questioning.

I don't think he ever saw art as a career. He wasn't interested in selling things. He was interested in creating them. He would give pictures away to family and friends, and be happy in the knowledge that they were getting something out of them. Also, he had a full-time job. And he had a family to support. And he had a family life that he enjoyed and valued above all else.

What's more, I don't think he saw a difference between the creativity he expressed in the many different areas of his life. A painting was just one exploration and expression of who he was and what he thought. But so was a curry cooked with care and love that he would share with the myriad of people who crammed into our house whenever there was a celebration to be had.

If one memory defines my view of my father's attitude to life it would be of him at any one of a number of parties at our house, standing slightly to the side of a room filled with people balancing plates of sublime food on their laps, and then throwing teasing conversational hand grenades into the fray just to get people talking, and laughing and thinking. Then, as debate raged, he would slip out of the room, smiling, to do the same thing somewhere else. And he, like my mother, would only eat last of all, after everyone else had.

Talking to people about him, I've lost count of the number of times I've been told that he encouraged them to follow their dreams. To not be bound by tradition. To think again about the world around them. And to choose their own path through it. I think that these conversations, and the seeds they planted, meant as much to him as any of the pictures he painted. After all, the conversations were about creativity and communication, just like the pictures.

Long ago I came to the conclusion that he thought the greatest work of art you could create was how you lived your life. And it was the greatest because it was the most immediate, and all-encompassing, and enjoyable. And also it was the only art form that was accessible, creatively, to everyone.

The only problem is that you can't put it in an art gallery and sell it. And we live in a commercial world. A world in which, if a price can't be put on something, then it's easy to assume that it has no value. But price is very rarely a good measure of worth. And it's often the unmeasurable things about a man that are the true measure of that man.

Even though Pop Art was a path that my father never chose to wander down, there was, in the early 1970s, a moment when he did seem to embrace some aspects of its enthusiasms. In particular, he started painting with bright, vibrant, almost acrylic colours. He used these colours for a large series of paintings he was creating for a specific exhibition. The exhibition was to be held in the building of the Architectural Association.

It was probably ten years or more since any new work of his had been exhibited, so it was a big deal. Of course, I didn't know this as I was still a fairly young kid. But I do remember him being up in his attic studio for long hours at a stretch working on the pictures. And as he was still doing his normal full-time job he was, no doubt, also up there when I was fast asleep in bed dreaming about *Space 1999* and Jenny Hanley off *Magpie* and whether I'd get a Chopper bike at Christmas.

In all, he must have done close on fifty paintings for this exhibition. Some were single canvases. Some were meant to be hung as a group of four. And then there was a series of twenty that were meant to be exhibited together on a single wall.

The colours were bright blues and reds and yellows and oranges. The painting was flat. The shapes bold. The subject matter was a very stylised meditation on the ancient texts and philosophies of Tantric sex. At the time, I didn't think much about the paintings. They were just more pictures that my dad had done that got hung all over the house. Occasionally when friends would come home with me after school, they would point and giggle at the odd 'willy' that could be spotted if you looked at some of the pictures from a certain angle. But, to be honest, the imagery was so abstracted that you needed a very 'imaginative' mind to discern anything lewd or objectionable in them. Even Mary Whitehouse, who was big at the time, would have been hard pushed to call for their banning.

Unfortunately, the Architectural Association wasn't run by anyone nearly as enlightened as Mary Whitehouse. When they discovered the nature of the paintings, and got to see some of them, they cancelled the exhibition. An exhibition that my father had been researching, and pondering on, and painting for, for well over a year.

As far as I know he never talked about how much of a disappointment this was. But he didn't pick up a brush again for almost ten years. And ten years is a long time in the life of an artist. I can't help but wonder what he might have created in those lost years. The picture from 1983 that's outside my attic room door is one from the time when he did finally start to paint again. And that's why I love it. I love its calmness. And its serenity. And its suggestion of rebirth.

But most of all I love it because my father painted it.

* * *

I thought about trying to have one of my father's pictures reproduced in this book, but decided against it. It would probably end up looking like nothing in particular and you'd be left wondering what all the fuss was about.

Instead there's this, something my brother recently found in a pile of family papers. It's a card on the back of which is written, 'This is your best friend wishing you a very happy birthday'. It was for my sixth birthday – a year older than my son is today. And, I think, it says as much about my father as anything else.

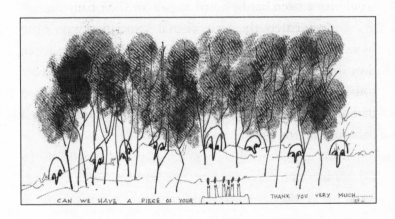

CAN WE HAVE A PIECE OF YOUR   THANK YOU VERY MUCH.........

* * *

I wouldn't say that I grew up in my brother's shadow, but I was aware that he cast a long one. In my eyes he was good at everything. He excelled at sport, passed exams with ease, and was always the leader of whatever gang coalesced around him. This was back in the days when gangs of kids were seen as something nearer to the *Just William* books than to South Central LA.

We would spend long summer afternoons playing football in the park. In the autumn half-term we'd bunk over the wall of the local cemetery and, armed with short sticks, take aim at the towering horse chestnut trees and claim the falling conkers as booty. Conkers that would either be pickled in vinegar or baked, or pickled in vinegar *and* baked, but still rarely make it above 'sixer' status. In the weeks up to the fifth of November we'd stuff old clothes with newspapers to make a lumpy dummy and sit outside the small parade of shops on the corner, accosting passers-by with: 'Penny for the guy, mister?'

I also remember being in awe of the party my parents let my brother have at home when he was a teenager. What sticks in my mind is the smell of Brut aftershave, trousers in brushed cotton that flared out at the bottoms like the base of a pyramid, and a Carpenters LP being constantly played on the family music centre. No doubt that's why, when I think about the painful magic of adolescent romance, the song that most comes to mind is not anything that played when I was in love, but my brother and his friends' sound-track of Karen Carpenter sweetly asking, 'Why do birds suddenly appear every time you are near?'

Firmly fixed in my mind are the large tins of what masqueraded as beer back then and gatecrashed a million celebrations under the name of Watney's Party Sevens. That was seven pints of watery fizz that started the evening as a barrel full of promises, but by the time you were clearing up the morning after contained nothing more than a thin puddle of disappointments and the floating torsos of count-less stubbed-out cigarettes.

All together now ... 'Just like me, they long to be, close to you'.

I looked up to my brother so much. But realising that I would never match up to him, I didn't try. I took two steps to the side and headed off in a different direction. Maybe that's why we ended up as quite different people. What occurs to me now is that even though we were quite close in age, and were raised by the same parents, in the same way, and lived through so many of the same experiences, we ended up looking at the passing parade through vastly different windows.

Looking back, the world is never purely as it was. The world is as we remember it. And each of us remembers it differently.

When it comes to my brother and food, three things stick in my mind. First, he really liked Heinz tomato ketchup. Any other ketchup was sacrilege. Second, he wasn't that keen on plain white rice. For him, white rice had to be deluged in lentils. And third, he loved my mother's apple chutney. Indeed, he did more than love it, he was a connoisseur of it. Every new batch of it that my mother cooked was tasted, tested and judged against the first batch that she had ever made, which had achieved an almost mystical status of perfection in his memory.

Mind you, he did have a point. The apple chutney was superb. All the more so because it was made from apples from the tree in our back garden. In my memory the tree was as tall as the clouds and as wide as the sky. But when I look at pictures of short-trousered and scabby-kneed me halfway up the disintegrating ladder that was propped patiently against it, I see that it was just a normal-sized apple tree. But under its branches we lit camp fires, we built dens, we played with Action Men and abandoned them like Japanese soldiers hiding in the jungle for years still thinking the war was going on. Then again, all children are careless generals. I find myself telling my own son, 'If you don't put your Thunderbirds away they're going to get lost.' At least, it's my voice, but it's my mother speaking, and I'm eight years old again, and under the apple tree, and more concerned with setting up my Hot Wheels track than putting away my Action Man. (Even if he did have gripping hands and realistic hair.)

The other thing to say about me and my brother and food is that, as pictures of the time clearly show, I was far fonder of food than he was. He had the build of a budding athlete, I had the build of a sprouting couch potato. Obviously, in the interests of making my childhood sound more tormented and stocking my young psyche with a shelf-ful of unresolved psychological issues that have resulted in me becoming the talented but troubled artiste you see before you today, I should really reveal that my bulging sweater shape was the result of endless comfort eating.

Unfortunately, this wasn't the case. I ate loads because I was greedy. And because my mother cooked wonderful food. Given those two facts it would have been silly not to. Indeed, in my opinion, it would have been positively rude not to regularly go back for second helpings. (And occasionally thirds.) And no one likes a rude boy.

Anyway, that's my story and I'm sticking to it.

So I grew up looking up to my brother. It wasn't quite 'On the day that you were born the angels got together and decided to create a dream come true', but it wasn't far off it.

Then again he supported Tottenham and I supported Leeds, so he couldn't have been that great.

It's strange to confront the possibility of your own non-existence. But investigate your past and you have to, time and time again. And it's hard to know how to react to the stories you uncover. A large part of it is a feeling of 'there but for the grace of God go I'. Another part of it is akin to the vicarious thrill that we get in recounting the fact that, for example, we 'were on the very train that crashed, just the day before!' For some reason, proximity to disaster, viewed from the armchair of hindsight, gives us both a shudder of fear and a life-affirming buzz.

But the possibility of non-existence takes these feelings a stage further. Because if, in the past, things had worked out differently for your parents, it wouldn't be a case of 'there but for the grace of God go I', because there would be no *I* to go.

Before I was born, before my brother was born, my father was dying. Not long married to my mother, with a home in a basement flat in Kensington, painting up a storm for an exhibition, he fell ill.

It started with a shallowness of breath. Then came a need to lie down straight after a day's work. Then a wheezing and gasping inability to walk across even the very small flat. He still needed to work, though, both to support the two of them, and also to save up for the house they were planning to buy. And he still needed to paint, because the exhibition was looming, and when you're struggling to get established as an artist, exhibitions don't come around that often.

Of course he went to the doctor's, but the doctor had no idea what was wrong with him. The tests he underwent in hospital didn't give any clues either. My mother was more worried than she'd ever been in her life. Not that she would have showed it. What my father thought I have no idea. But he wasn't the kind of person to wallow in an illness. When he had been growing up you didn't have the chance to do that. You just got on with it and got better. Only this time there seemed to be no better in sight.

It all came to a head on the day of the exhibition. The paintings were finished and delivered to the gallery. My parents were dressed up and ready to go to the opening. And then my father tried to walk across the living room of the flat, which doubled as his studio, to pick up his coat. He took three steps and collapsed. Lying on the floor, all breath seemed to have escaped him. With wracking heaves of his chest he had to fight for air. Half holding him, half dragging him, my mother got my father back into bed. She rang the gallery and told them he wouldn't be able to come to the opening of his own show, and then she rang for an ambulance that took him to Brompton Hospital.

Many days later he was released. His condition had stabilised, but he wasn't better. The doctor told my parents that he didn't know what the problem was. So he didn't know what could be done. And he feared that things could only get worse.

'So what should we do?' my mother asked.

'Go home,' the doctor said.

He didn't mean to the flat in Kensington. He meant to Ceylon. And he didn't mean that he thought it might help my father get better. He meant that if you're going to die, it's better that you're with your family.

My parents didn't have any spare money to buy tickets to Ceylon. All they had was two years of hard-earned savings that they'd assiduously put aside so they'd eventually have enough to put down as a deposit on a house.

But now the prospect of a house seemed a dim and distant and heartbreakingly poignant dream. So they cashed in their dream and bought tickets for a boat that would carry my father home on his last journey. Of course, they didn't talk about it in those terms, but the very fact that they were abandoning everything they had worked so hard to achieve shows that thoughts of my father's impending death were travel companions who'd booked into the same cabin, and would seek them out wherever they went on the boat.

Three days out of Southampton, my father started to pick up. By the time the boat reached the Suez Canal, he was teasing my mother by chatting to other women. As the boat docked in Colombo, he was back to his old self.

When the shock and joy and sheer unexpectedness of the recovery wore off, my parents went to see a doctor. They went through the symptoms, the tests, the inability of the British doctors to diagnose the problem, and the incredible turn around in my father's health on the boat back to Ceylon. The doctor asked them to come back in a couple of days when he'd had a chance to think about it all. When they returned, he gave his diagnosis.

He said that not many people die for their art, but my father had been about to become one of them. The problem, it seems, was that in order to get the paintings ready for the upcoming exhibition, my father had been working long into the night. And the basement flat had little ventilation. And the nights were cold so all the windows were kept closed. And the paints that he'd been using had a lead base.

In effect, his paintings had been killing him.

Once on the boat, sailing away from the English Channel and round into the Mediterranean, the sea air had cleaned out the residue of the poisonous fumes that had accumulated in his lungs and he was able to breathe properly again.

My parents stayed in Ceylon for almost a year, but there was no work for my father. In the 1950s, Britain was still rebuilding after the war so anyone with architectural experience could easily find employment. Ceylon was different. There was nowhere near as much building work to be done. And if you didn't have the right qualifications, or the right friends, what work there was would never come your way. So, reluctantly, my parents caught a boat back to England, with almost no money in their pockets, to start again. Again.

Not long after they set up home in England for a second time, my brother was born. I followed a little over two years later.

When I first started thinking about the dates of all these events, I went and checked the date of the picture outside my attic room door: 1957. It was one of the paintings that my father had been working on at the time he collapsed. At the time that he almost died.

So when I stare into its swirling vortex of pitch-black brushstrokes, my feelings about it are somewhat confused. I like the picture. I admire the picture. I even love the picture. But I'm also afraid of it. Because somewhere at the back of that vortex, I don't exist.

ten
and a half

A BRIEF HISTORY OF CURRY
IN BRITAIN: PART THREE

No history of curry in Britain could be complete without mention of the partition of India in August 1947. Astronomers couldn't agree whether the fourteenth or fifteenth of August was the most auspicious date for India's freedom, so midnight between the two dates was chosen as the moment. As Nehru put it, 'At the stroke of the midnight hour, when the world sleeps, India will wake up to life and freedom.' Unfortunately, India also woke up to unresolvable differences between the Hindu majority and the Muslim minority. Jinnah, leader of the Muslims, insisted on a separate state. Hence the creation of Pakistan. Further complicating matters was the fact that Pakistan was split into two separate parts separated by hundreds of miles. As the new borders solidified, it is estimated that ten million Hindus, Muslims and Sikhs fled their homes and relocated. It is also thought that in the turmoil between 500,000 and 1,000,000 people died in inter-communal violence. Little wonder then that many people wanted to escape abroad. In addition, in East Pakistan, the country that is now Bangladesh, the economic prospects were far from good. This was the same region that contains Sylhet, from where many merchant seamen had come. So the tradition of leaving the country to work was firmly embedded. But what also changed in the days of unrest was that it wasn't just the labourers who felt the urge to get out. Students who had been involved in political protest also realised that staying where they were might not be their best option. Many of them came to Britain.

Arriving in a new country and finding work was, as ever, difficult. Today, for newcomers, the first rung on the employment ladder is hand-washing cars, or delivering pizza flyers door to door. Back then the only real option would have been casual labour in restaurants. They'd work long, unsocial hours as kitchen porters or cleaners. It was all cash in hand, no questions asked, and keep your head down and do the work. But all the while as they slogged their guts out for next to nothing many of them were learning, from the bottom up, how restaurants operated. So when they'd saved enough money from their meagre wages, and were trying to figure out how to reach the next rung on the ladder, it was only natural to pool resources with a few others and take the leap into the dark of trying to set up the only business of which they had any real experience.

It was always going to be an uphill struggle, but, looking back, they had many things going for them that might just make the dream possible. For a start, they weren't afraid of hard work. Many had begun their working lives toiling in the bowels of ocean-going steam ships. Portering in restaurants wasn't exactly a stroll in the park either. So when they got the chance to work for themselves, you knew that they wouldn't fail through lack of effort.

Then, they had a tight support network of fellow immigrants around them. It is estimated that at one point 80 per cent of all Indian restaurants in London were run by people originally from Sylhet. That they were single men, or had families out of the country, meant that their sole focus could be on making their fledgling businesses a success. Having often started out working in the same restaurants meant they had first-hand experience of a successful template. This is why even today you can walk into almost any Indian restaurant, in any high street, in any part of the country, and find not only the same menu, but also the same decor as one hundreds of miles away.

The food that is the typical curry-house scoff is based on common roots from Bangladesh. Of course, it has evolved and adapted to the British palate, but its traditions originate in Sylhet. The ubiquitous flock wallpaper was originally an attempt to echo the high-class restaurants which themselves had sought to recreate the feel of the luxurious clubhouses found in India under the British Raj. How much this resonated with, for example, someone wandering into the Taj Mahal on Tooting High Street in the 1960s and 1970s is hard to tell, but the look became part of the experience. As did subdued lighting and unsubdued sitars. Of course, the other thing about flock wallpaper was that it was generally falling from favour and there wasn't that much demand for it any more, so they could probably get it cheap. In addition, many of the restaurants were fitted out by the same firm of decorators, and no doubt they had a job lot of the stuff in a lock-up somewhere.

But maybe the biggest factor that gave the people who opened the early restaurants an edge is, bizarrely, that they weren't very good cooks. Why this was an advantage is twofold. To begin with, whatever they cooked had to be relatively simple to prepare. The elaborations and exquisite regional variations that you find raved about in reviews of the new breed of Indian restaurants today were, largely, beyond them. Instead they used relatively few ingredients, and cooked what they cooked quickly. If you're running a restaurant both these factors are, financially, a godsend. And as they had no great aspirations as chefs, they had no great desire to fiddle with a winning formula. Once they discovered what people liked, they pretty much stuck to it.

The actual cooking process was further simplified when the sauce-based approach was developed. This enabled a wide variety of final dishes to be prepared from common sauces to which different meat, vegetables or spices were added. Again, for a restaurateur whose profits accumulate only from very small margins, this was vitally important.

When you add all these things together, I believe there is only one conclusion you can draw. Namely that, long before McDonald's muscled in on the scene, the curry house was, and is, one of the first and most successful restaurant franchises in the country. It hit on a formula the public grew to love, then offered the same food, the same decor and the same experience in countless branches across the land. But what makes the curry house a better franchise than all the rest is that it isn't centrally owned. So the profits really do go to the people who run the places.

But the common franchise feel of the curry house wasn't just of benefit to the restaurant owners. It also helped acclimatise a whole generation of new customers to the joys of eating out. In the 1960s Britain's economy started to boom. The post-war recession was receding in memory and the man in the street began to find himself with the odd pound in his pocket that he could afford to spend on things he wanted, not just things he needed. For the first time a mass of people were discovering that they had disposable income. Eating out became an option. However, for many people it was still a somewhat uncomfortable prospect. But if you could go to a restaurant where you knew what you were going to get, knew that you were going to like it, and knew what it would cost, then the whole endeavour had some of the uncertainty removed – so you could just concentrate on having a good time.

The context all this was going on in bears a little consideration too. Throughout the 1960s and 1970s, and all the way into the 1980s, there existed within Britain three main competing views of Indianness. First, there was the considerable hangover from the days of the Raj. You only had to look at the popularity of the writing of authors like M.M. Kaye, E.M. Forster and Paul Scott to realise that. *The Jewel in the Crown* on ITV also proved a ratings winner. But the less said about David Lean's *A Passage to India* the better. And I say that as someone whose favourite film is *Lawrence of Arabia*. My problem with the film set in India is Alec Guinness. An Alec Guinness who blacked up to play an Indian. Laughable though such an idea now is – and, indeed, should have been at the time – it is a bit of casting that is a perfect metaphor for the still lingering colonial attitude to India: that is, in order to do justice to the complexity of an Indian character like Professor Godbole, you really need a British actor.

India was exotic, India was glamorous and, apparently, India was at its best when the British had been in charge. As Britain as a whole was still trying to redefine itself in a fast-changing world, nostalgia for the Raj exerted a very potent pull.

If the Raj was the establishment view of India, there also existed a counter-culture view. This got its biggest boost when John, Paul, George and Ringo went walkabout. When the Beatles hotfooted it to the subcontinent for a spot of meditation with the Maharishi, all things Indian became the very cutting edge of hip. And it was an encounter that added mysticism and spirituality (and lentils) to India's growing appeal.

There was, of course, an alternative view to the alternative view. This was that Indians were funny. Not just funny strange, but funny ha-ha. Peter Sellers blacking up as an

Indian doctor peddled a line in it in a film with Sophia Loren. Spike Milligan often had an Indian character up his sleeve that would combine mockery and cruelty. And the Carry On team came to a characteristically sticky end up the Khyber Pass. (F'nar, f'nar.) On TV the key perpetrators of Asian stereotyping were the 'comedians' on an ITV show *The Comedians*, the BBC's *It Ain't Half Hot, Mum*, and the 'hilarious' *Mind Your Language* which managed to effort-lessly ridicule and offend every single ethnic group in the country in every single episode.

Unfortunately, hanging over all these three views was the sword of Damocles that the Conservative politician and Shadow Cabinet member Enoch Powell unsheathed in his infamous 1968 'Rivers of Blood' speech. The gist of his argument was that 'coloured' immigration to Britain was a disaster waiting to happen. He stated that in 'fifteen or twenty years' time the black man will have the whip hand over the white man'. And that if nothing was done to control the situation then Britain's rivers would flow with blood. Even more unfortunately it was a line of 'reasoning' that found considerable favour with certain segments of the population. Hence the rise of violent right-wing skinheads. And the worryingly popular pastime of 'paki-bashing'. (Of which I had first-hand experience – or, more accurately, first-boot experience.)

Combine all these things together and you have some idea of the social context in the 1960s and 1970s. And that was the context I grew up in. Looking back, what I find most striking is that none of these three overlapping views of Indianness had any relevance at all to me. Or indeed to the majority of Asians in Britain. What had the Raj, or drug-fuelled counter-culture mysticism, or head-wobbling caricatures, or mythical rivers of blood to do with any of us? But this was the context that we existed in. And this was the context within which Indian restaurants would somehow climb to their position of prominence and esteem within the culinary landscape of Britain.

The other key factor was, of course, the assassination of Archduke Ferdinand on a road leading out of Sarajevo in 1914.

eleven

I BRING YOU FRANKINCENSE

My father had one sister. She worked in Colombo as a secretary until 1956. Then she followed him to London. After that she worked in Germany and the Netherlands and travelled extensively in Europe and the United States.

For all the time I can remember her, she worked and lived with Harry, a Dutch Catholic priest.

This, I realise, sounds a little strange. But had you met them you would have rapidly come to the conclusion that there was nothing odd about the situation at all. There was nothing physical about their relationship, they were just two people whose ideas, ideals and spirits meshed together and complemented each other on some level that the rest of us can probably only hope for.

When I think about my aunt, I think about the times we went to visit them at their flat in the Netherlands. And I think about her cooking. What follows is a recipe for a dish I always associate with her. It is for a Ceylonese speciality called seeni sambol. So intense is the flavour in this particular sambol that you could eat it on its own with plain rice and not feel short-changed.

SEENI SAMBOL

50g dried Maldive fish
10 curry leaves
3 cardamom pods, bruised
1 cinnamon stick
3 cloves
10cm-piece rampe (leaf of the pandanus tree)
5cm-piece lemongrass
100ml vegetable oil
500g onions, sliced
2 teaspoons chilli powder
salt, to taste
2 teaspoons sugar
80g tamarind pulp, soaked in 350ml warm water

Soak the Maldive fish in a little warm water overnight. Drain and crush the fish into small pieces. Fry the curry leaves, cardamom, cinnamon, cloves, rampe and lemongrass in the oil over medium heat for 5 minutes. Turn the heat down, add the onions and chilli powder and fry gently until the onions are browned. Add the Maldive fish, salt and sugar and fry for a further 7 minutes. Keep stirring so that nothing sticks and burns. Strain the liquid from the tamarind, discarding the pulp, and add the liquid to the pan. Simmer for 2 minutes. Remove lemongrass and cinnamon stick before serving.

Seeni sambol translates roughly as 'sugar sambol'. But in the mouth the sugar hit is married to a fiery heat and a tamarind sourness. Whenever I eat it I am immediately transported back to my aunt's dining table. Actually, come to think of it, the dining table rarely featured as a place to sit down and eat as usually there were so many people around for the meals that you would have to find what space you could, anywhere in the room, and camp out with your plate balanced on your lap. Most of the other people were students, as Harry and my aunt did a lot of work with students, both from overseas and indigenous, wherever they went.

It was Harry's work with students in the 1950s that played a major part in radicalising him. As a child in the Netherlands he had watched as the German tanks rolled, implacably, into his home town, and his father had been interned at Buchenwald as a hostage, so his earliest impressions of international relations were far from positive. Then as a young priest he was assigned to work with Indonesian students who travelled to the Netherlands to study. From these encounters a different world-view started to emerge. A world-view based on exchange and equality that he held dear all his life.

As I've mentioned earlier, Harry also played a major part in my parents' story. And, indeed, he presided over their wedding.

Harry travelled extensively in the east and everywhere he went he absorbed and assimilated as much of the culture as he could. He came to believe that the consumerist, arrogant, western approach to life and the world was not the only, and far from the best, way forward.

Had his temperament been different, he might have led headline-grabbing revolutions. Instead, the revolutions he worked for were on a far smaller and more human scale. Later on in his life, for example, angered by the inequity of many aspects of the international trade system, he took very practical steps to do something about it. He helped set up in Sri Lanka an organisation that supported and encouraged small producers of goods to become more independent and self-reliant. A central facet of the project was a spice farm. That's because even today the people who grow spices and work in spice production are often woefully underpaid for their labours. Of course, by the time the spices appear on the shelves of the supermarkets, massive mark-ups have been imposed on them. But very little of the price you and I pay over the counter ever filters its way down to the people who actually grow the stuff.

Strange to think that the very same kind of price hikes are still in place now as when European traders first headed out east in search of spices. The only thing is that back then maybe things were more honest. Getting spices home from the east was a hazardous business. Often they would have to pass through the hands of myriad traders before they arrived in Europe. And each would need to take a little profit. Nowadays the hazards are few, and there aren't anywhere near as many traders in the chain. But maybe the profits being made are as great. They're just concentrated into fewer hands.

My aunt's ability as a cook, and Harry's radical world-view, coalesced in a cookbook they wrote. It was a low-budget affair called *The Spice of Happiness* and there was as much philosophy in it as there was cooking. While my aunt handled the recipe side of things, Harry went off at angles and explored the lessons he had learned from the Asian approach to, and philosophical contemplation of, cooking and eating food.

One of the themes he was particularly fond of concerned the community that forms whenever food is prepared. He saw this as a challenge to, and criticism of, the western way of sharing food, in which all too often you go round to someone's house only after all the preparation has been done. Then the cook scurries round the kitchen while the guests wait, often in another room, and only see the food when it arrives on their plates.

In contrast to this, Harry was very taken with the way that even in the smallest of eastern communities, when there is a celebration to be had, everyone pitches in and prepares the food together. In the commonality of purpose, and the sharing of what otherwise might be seen as repetitive chores, the bonds of the community would be formed and strengthened. Then when everyone sat down to eat the meal, somehow it meant more, and they enjoyed it more.

Despite the habits of contemporary western entertaining, it is a process of which, I believe, we all still possess some deep-rooted folk memory. Why else, when you do go round to someone's house for dinner, do you inevitably feel the pull of the kitchen? And when you see the host hard at work, you want to help. But the social niceties of the situation all too often have the host turning down the offers of assistance. Because we're stuck in the mindset that the rules of hospitality demand that we wait on our guests.

Maybe it's time we consigned such thinking to the bin, and the next time we invite someone round to eat, suggest that they come early and help us cook. After all, isn't that approach to things part of the reason why people like barbecues? The accepted social rules of entertaining are broken down and the ensuing informality helps everyone relax and enjoy. And everyone pitches in.

A more direct gauge of the philosophical view Harry espoused can be seen in this extract from *The Spice of Happiness*.

It is strange to observe the change in eating habits in prosperous countries, against the ones practised in the so-called poor ones. A look at a modern kitchen in the west gives the impression that it is geared to feeding fairly large groups of people on many occasions. All the amenities are there. In actual practice, all this expensive gear is seldom used, in comparison to its extent and the money invested. These elaborate kitchens are used to cut down the time for cooking to a minimum, not to promote kitchen culture. The accumulation of things is nowhere better shown than in the fully equipped modern kitchen, that does not serve hospitality and sharing, but is only geared to saving time – for what? Even smells suffer in the process: they are sucked away mechanically, much to the dismay of the stomach, which loses its companion, the nose, for the enjoyment and digestion of food.

You have to admit he's got a point. He also had a point when he used to object to the term 'Third World'. He'd say that there was only One World, and we all lived in it together. So we better learn how to get on.

I'm also reminded of his original take on things by the sermon he shared with us at my brother's wedding. Harry took as his text the wedding feast at Canaan. Basically Jesus was a guest at a wedding when the wine ran out. This was a grave crisis and reflected very poorly on the family hosting the bash. Jesus sorted the problem by turning water into wine. (Which is a fairly useful trick to have up your sleeve). Even from my dim and distant church-going days I remember that the wedding feast at Canaan was afforded such prominence and significance because it was given as Jesus' very first miracle. Harry came at the story from a different angle. He approached it from the bride's point of view. After all, here she was, on the biggest day in her life, and she gets upstaged by a guest. Not the best start to a marriage.

Most of the time when we went to see my aunt and Harry they were living in the Netherlands, so along with the curries, chutneys and sambols, when I think of her cooking I also conjure up visions of all kinds of salamis and strong, dry cheeses. But above all, I remember chocolate milk. I'm sure chocolate milk was around in London when I was growing up, but I never came across it. Occasionally a box of Nesquik would appear in a cupboard, but that wasn't at all the same. With Nesquik you had to mix the powder yourself into the milk. And I was never patient enough to get all the powder to dissolve, so my memory of drinking Nesquik is of a pale beige liquid with small chocolate-powder globules floating on the surface. The chocolate milk in the Netherlands was different. It came in a glass bottle. All you had to do was take off the foil top and pour it into a glass. And it was thick. Really thick. It didn't pour, it glugged. It was so rich that you couldn't drink a lot of it in one go. But that didn't stop me trying.

Reading through the book that my aunt and Harry wrote, I came across another recipe that had memories glugging back. It's for sandwich spread. Only it isn't the kind of sandwich spread you've probably ever encountered before.

SANDWICH SPREAD

125g grated cheese
6 green chillies, seeded and finely sliced
1 teaspoon butter

Mix well with fork into a smooth paste. Spread mixture onto buttered bread.

* * *

Start thinking about food and growing up and you can find yourself wandering into some very odd kitchens. You watch the cooks at work, you see the ingredients being prepared and you peer into the oven to try to see what's being cooked. Then the oven door is opened and you recoil from the blast of heat. Finally the dish is ready and as you stare at it you can't help thinking, 'Did I really eat that?'

Spam fritters, for instance. Whatever happened to spam fritters? Or the top of the milk from a doorstep-delivered bottle snaffled up as soon as you woke and before the blue tits had the chance to peck their way through the silver foil lids. Whatever happened to the top of the milk? And, incidentally, now that no one gets their milk delivered to the doorstep any more, what do the blue tits put on their early morning cornflakes? And if there are no milk deliveries, then there are no milkmen, so who do bored housewives have affairs with now? No wonder we're surrounded by flat-chested blue tits and *Desperate Housewives* is the most popular show on TV with women, now that George Clooney has long since left *ER*.

The same shape as a spam fritter, but with an entirely different significance, was the small, white wafer that every Sunday morning the priest in the church at the top of our road would place on my tongue, solemnly whispering to me the constantly worrying revelation that it was 'the body of Christ'.

As you walked back to your pew with your head reverentially bowed, you were supposed to be quietly contemplating the profundity of the exchange. However, as

I walked back with the Host dissolving on my tongue, I couldn't help contemplating how much its texture reminded me of the sherbet-filled flying saucers you could get from the sweetshop for only tuppence a bag. But the 'body of Christ' didn't give you the small boy's crack-cocaine equivalent fizzing hit of sherbet you'd get when your tongue first breached the frankly feeble hull of the flying saucer. But maybe it should have done. If only the Vatican had developed a Host that contained just a tiny blister of sherbet, maybe all the problems they were having 'attracting young people to the Church' would have gone out of the stained-glass window. After all, even the most lacklustre of droning sermonisers could have drawn the analogy between the fizz in your mouth when the sherbet enters it, and the fizz in your soul when God enters there.

As you can tell, I probably wasn't the most devout Asian Roman Catholic in 1970s South London. Mind you, there weren't many of us about. There was, essentially, me and my brother. Of course, my mother also came with us to church, but because she was of Portuguese descent her complexion was relatively fair. The only really dark faces I'd see at church were a few West Indians, or the occasional African priest who might be visiting the parish. The majority of the rest of the parishioners seemed to be Irish.

My father, who had the almost mahogany colour of the tropics about him, stopped coming to church with us relatively early on. When my mother quizzed him about this he said, 'Why do I need to go to church? Everywhere that I am is my church.' It was a very good line, and now, thirty years later, I know exactly what he meant. However, when I, as an eleven-year-old boy, tried the line out on the headmaster of my enthusiastically Roman Catholic primary school one Monday morning, having bunked off the previous Sunday's mass in order to play football down the park, it didn't have quite the same ring of profundity about it. Oh well, at least I got the chance to practise my handwriting every playtime for the rest of that week. (Do schoolchildren still get 'lines'? Or has that long since gone the way of Roneod worksheets and free school milk?)

As most of the school was filled with Irish children, so most of our friends seemed to be called O'Something or FitzWhatsit. Back in the 1970s, being Irish didn't have the cachet that it does now. Back in the 1970s being Irish was, for many English people, associated with the Troubles and the IRA. It was a time a million miles away from the Corrs and *Riverdance*, and Oirish-themed bars where everyone's welcome for the craic. Not that any of the tensions filtered down to primary-school level. If the prejudices were to really hit my schoolmates, it would happen when they were young men and out looking for work and getting stopped on the streets for no reason at all. And by then I'd lost touch with most of them.

Funny how things go round in circles. It used to be the Irish who were viewed as in league with terrorists. Now it's the Muslims' turn. Maybe all we need to get people seeing sense is a Muslim version of the Corrs to conquer the charts, and for *Bellydance! The Musical* to sell out at the Albert Hall for two dancetastic months. But, unfortunately, for obvious reasons Oislamic-themed bars are a bit of a non-starter.

If there was a commonality between my family and the Irish families around us it was probably in an underlying sense of otherness. Also, the things that they held dear were the same ones that we did. Family was important. And so was religion. They are, I suppose, the social superglue of immigrant communities everywhere.

When my mother arrived in Britain after the war, with her parents and siblings, they knew hardly anyone. The Catholic Church gave them an immediate introduction into a community. It hastened their integration into the new world they found themselves in. Whatever criticisms you might make of the Catholic Church (and there are many to be made), it welcomed newcomers to its fold with open arms. Well, as opened arms as you could expect in a still largely socially repressed Britain. And it wasn't in the details of theology that the newcomers found common ground with their 'hosts', but in the sharing of rituals.

For my mother and her parents, Britain was indeed a strange, and largely unwelcoming, world. They didn't know their way around it, they didn't know how it worked, and they were yet to fathom out its complex social rules. The Church, however, was different. They knew how the Church worked. They knew what to expect from it. And they knew what it expected from them. While I would hesitate to say that it played as central a role in their lives as it had in the east, it did help them to stay centred.

As for me, I was a generation down the line, so the

Church never meant anywhere near as much. But even though I can't say that I ever 'believed' more than I had to, religion was nonetheless important. I suppose you can't sit through all those sermons, for all those years, and not pick up some kind of moral map by which you try to navigate your life. My other legacy is a generalised feeling of guilt. It's a Catholic thing. We were taught that from the very moment we are born we have 'original sin'. And we were taught that when we do bad things we had to confess them to a priest and he would be able to tell us what penance to perform so that we could be absolved of our guilt. While I've long since given up going to confession, I'm afraid the whole guilt thing has proved far harder to shake off. So most of the time, about most things, I feel, to varying degrees, guilty.

The bizarre thing about going to confession is that you start doing it when you're about nine or ten. You're supposed to do it every week. The problem is that at nine or ten you don't actually do that much that is wrong. So you find yourself in the confessional with very little to say. But the priest is waiting on the other side of the grille and you don't want to let him down and waste his time. So you make stuff up. You invent sins to be forgiven for. Which, especially when you consider that lying is a sin, rather seems to defeat the point of the whole exercise.

The other thing I remember about being a brown-skinned Roman Catholic in a 1970s primary school is that you always tended to get the same part in the nativity play. You invariably ended up being one of the three kings.

Sometimes you brought frankincense, sometimes you brought myrrh and sometimes you brought gold. But there was never any chance of playing Joseph. That's because the commonly held belief at the time was that Jesus looked like Robert Powell, so his dad (even if it was his adopted dad) would look similar too. Especially as his mum (his real mum, impregnated in some kind of immaculate early IVF-and-surrogacy deal) was always played by the prettiest Irish girl in the class.

Actually, I didn't mind being one of the kings. The kings got to wear the best clothes. Not for me the hastily remodelled and stitched blankets of the shepherds. No, I was always arrayed in silken finery. Which was nice. Years later my father's brother sent us an article that had just appeared in the *Ceylon Times*. It was about recent research that linked one of the legendary three kings with the Chettiars, a community of traders that had started off in India and then moved to Ceylon. The article went on to list the names of families descended from this community. Among them was the name of 'Candappa'. It is, I know, a tenuous claim. But it is a claim so outrageous it would be churlish of me not to make it. And if I say so myself, there was always a certain regal quality that could never be totally obscured by my somewhat squeaky voice as I delivered the line, 'I bring you frankincense.'

Whenever I told anyone that I was Catholic, they would initially be a little confused. I had a brown skin so, by rights, I should have been Hindu, or Sikh, or Muslim. Roman Catholic didn't really fit in with the preconceived ideas of the time. I would inevitably have to start explaining about my mother being of Portuguese descent, at which point the listener's eyes would glaze over. So I'd stop explaining and switch the topic of conversation to something else. I suppose what I was encountering was a dislocation between who I was expected to be and who I actually was.

It happens a lot. But I'm used to it by now.

twelve

TWO MEALS

The most memorable meal I ever cooked was Chinese. There was steamed trout, stir-fried vegetables, rice and even a packet of fortune cookies I'd found in a Chinese supermarket off Shaftesbury Avenue. There was also a bottle of sake that would be warmed in a dish of piping hot water and then poured into small ceramic cups. As it turns out, we never got round to drinking the sake.

I wasn't cooking a Chinese meal because of deeply significant multicultural reasons to do with my diverse cultural heritage, but because I rather fancied a Chinese. And I hoped the person I was cooking for would also fancy a Chinese too. There was a time when I had hoped she'd also fancy something else, but not any more. This is that evening's recipe.

CHINESE STEAMED TROUT
SERVES 4

1 tablespoon sesame seed oil
1 tablespoon light soy sauce
1 tablespoon dry sherry
2 rainbow trout
4 cloves garlic, thinly sliced
6 spring onions
2 x 2.5cm pieces ginger, shredded
2 tablespoons dry white vermouth
2 tablespoons vegetable oil

Mix together the sesame seed oil, soy sauce and sherry and use to brush the inside and the skin of the fish. Mix together garlic, spring onions and ginger and put a quarter of the mixture inside each fish. Place the fish in foil, scatter over the rest of garlic mixture and pour over the vermouth and the oil. Put in a steamer and steam for 15 minutes or until the fish is tender.

Arrange the fish on a warmed serving plate, spoon over the juices and serve immediately.

Obviously, I didn't use the vermouth. Mainly because I knew I'd never drink the rest of it if I got a whole bottle and used just the two tablespoons required. But also because vermouth is a word I just couldn't, and still can't, take seriously. It's not as bad as Malibu, but decidedly worse than Martini. It's the kind of word that Roger Moore's James

Bond might just have got away with, but had it issued from the lips of Sean Connery you'd be a tad concerned as to just how good this particular Bond flick was going to be. Either way it was a word that cut very little ice in New Cross where I lived at the time.

Explaining about New Cross, even to fellow Londoners, is never easy. For most people it's just a place you might drive through if you were heading east to the Essex riviera of Clacton and Southend. By way of illumination I would refer anyone who asked to the Monopoly board. On the Monopoly board the cheapest place you can buy is the Old Kent Road. Well, drive along the Old Kent Road, in the wrong direction, and keep ploughing on as it peters out, and eventually you'll end up in New Cross. I was living there because it was cheap. And it was cheap because it was rough.

At the time, though no one really knew it, the most significant thing about New Cross was Goldsmiths' College. It was at Goldsmiths' College around about then that the likes of Damien Hirst were studying. In my opinion Mr Hirst's work is often misinterpreted. It is derided as being 'conceptual' rubbish. Obviously these misguided critics never lived in New Cross. Especially, long before it was 'done up'. Had they done so, they'd realise that Hirst was only faithfully representing the things that he saw.

A shark suspended in dodgy-looking liquid? A fish stall at Deptford market, five minutes' walk from New Cross, on any Saturday. Gaudy 'spin' pictures that splash colour all over a canvas? Sunday morning, outside any of the pubs after the Goths have overdosed on snakebite and kebabs the night before. And a show cabinet full of neatly displayed proprietary medicines and drugs? What's that if not a super-realistic artistic response to a bleary-eyed stagger into Patel's the Chemist's in search of a box of Anadin Extra to cure a raging hangover? No, his work isn't conceptual. It is all still life. It's just not from any life that usually gets stilled.

As for Mr Hirst's involvement in the unofficial England football song 'Vindaloo', well, that needs no explanation at all in terms of its artistic genesis in New Cross. Especially as the lovely Millwall are only a stone's throw away up the siren-wailing road.

So there I was in New Cross with two trout and a steamer. I was cooking dinner for a young woman I had been at university with. A young woman I had been at university with and, for a brief period, been besotted by. I'll call her M.

I met M in that bizarre, unrepeatable time that is anyone's first term away from home in the hotbed of acade-mia. (You sincerely hope it is going to be more hotbed than academia.) You're making a whole brand new circle of friends, you're living away from your parents, and you're even having to do all your own washing. All the while your raging libido is convinced that 'this is it, THIS IS IT'. At the time I was at university, the lush splendour of *Brideshead Revisited* was weekly bewitching a nation on the TV. So being a student was glamorous. The only problem was that *Brideshead Revisited* was set among the dreaming spires of 1930s Oxford. And I was going to university in

1980s Reading. We didn't have dreaming spires. We had the Butts Shopping Centre. An aptly named edifice if ever there was one.

M came from Cornwall where her family owned land and ran a farm. For some reason I've always had it in my head that they owned half of Cornwall. Obviously they didn't, and it was probably just me back-projecting that whole Brideshead thing onto my life in order to make it more romantic. She was also very pretty, bohemian, had a wickedly irreverent sense of humour and wore fetchingly accessorised Andy Pandy-style dungarees. So what chance did a simple Sarf Lunnun boy have?

Actually, as it turned out, no chance at all. That's because she rapidly got off with Martin, who combined Liverpudlian working-class credentials with the world-weary charm of someone who'd spent a gap year in the States. This was way back before gap years had been invented. On top of all that he knew about people like Sartre and Camus. (And how to pronounce them.) And marijuana. He knew about marijuana.

Like I said, I didn't stand a chance.

Bloody hell, if only I'd been gay I'd have tried to get off with him myself. Instead I just hung out with him. And M. And also Pauline, my first encounter with the Geordie diaspora, who, once I'd stopped spending endless post-student-union-disco sessions moping in my room till the early hours listening to the likes of Rose Royce's 'Love Don't Live Here Anymore' and writing really, really, really bad poetry about the M situation, I discovered was fantastic.

So, after I'd come to my senses, and had scratched the Rose Royce single to buggery anyway, I started going out with Pauline.

In so doing I'd managed to extricate myself from the unbearably painful and somewhat clichéd experience of the Love Triangle and embarked upon the remarkably artistically ignored social set-up of the Love Parallelogram. You know, four friends, two couples, with one relationship always slightly ahead of the other. Historically speaking, it's a set-up that has always proved far less destructive than the Love Triangle. Unless, of course, you're a member of Abba.

I remember it as being a time in my life that was incredibly intense. But when I try to pin down specifics, I can fix on next to nothing that actually happened. I have an image in my head of sitting on Martin's bed one drink-stained night in our hall of residence, early on in the whole farrago, as he told me that he really fancied M and what did I think he should do? I, who was at the time besotted with her, advised him to ask her out. Why the hell did I do that? Mind you, I got a shed-load of self-pitying 'poetry' out of that one. And I remember all of us one Sunday going to nearby Twyford to visit the zoo. Only to find that the zoo we were looking for was actually in Twycross.

Heady days.

After we left university we went our separate ways. But, given the evidence of our Twyford/Twycross debacle, it could very easily have been that we all went the same way, but our senses of direction were so crap that we all ended up in completely different places.

But we did, after a fashion, stay in touch with each other. Which is how I came to have invited M over to dinner in New Cross (who wouldn't be tempted?) one Sunday evening. I think it was the weekend of the August bank holiday. She was, at the time, working for *Vogue*. Which sounded very glamorous. I, at the time, was working on an advertising campaign for corn plasters. Which was not in the least glamorous. Oh well, I could always console myself with the thought that without the corn plaster ads, magazines like *Vogue* wouldn't make enough money to pay for all those glossy fashion shoots. Except that corn plaster ads tended to run in *The Lady*. Or *Woman's Weekly*.

Anyway, I wanted the evening to go perfectly. Not that I harboured any lingering hopes of rekindling even the slightest of romantic flames. That particular Elvis had long since left the building. No, I just wanted the evening to go well because I wanted the evening to go well. Of course, long after the meal was finished and M had gone home and I was in suds up to my elbows, I might allow myself a wistful muse or two. Because though I might have the exterior of a cynical adman (though obviously not the salary to match or I wouldn't be living in New Cross), I did still possess just a sliver of the soul of the love-torn poet. Or should that be 'poet'? Yes, I think it probably should.

The doorbell rang as I was stuffing garlic, spring onions and ginger into the belly of the fish. I ran downstairs, opened the door, and gave M a big hug. Unfortunately, I'd forgotten that I had been stuffing garlic, spring onions and ginger into the belly of a fish. Not the best start to the evening. But a couple of glasses of chilled white wine soon sorted things out. That was a couple of glasses of chilled white wine for me, as M wasn't drinking. As I fast-forwarded to see what this might mean for how the evening would pan out, the bottle of sake waiting in the kitchen started to take on a strange air of foreboding.

By now M was in the living room of the flat (which was also the dining room of the flat) and sitting on the hand-me-down sofa I'd got from my uncle that converted into a bed. (That was the sofa that converted into a bed, not my uncle.) The sofa itself had seen better days (and presumably nights) but luckily for me at the time the 'throw' craze was just about getting up a full head of steam. And I'd even got some carnations in a vase on the table. All I had to do now was put on the right record (you remember records?) to set the right ambience, and then I could retire to the kitchen to chop up the stir-fry. I think I selected 'Gymnopédies' by Satie. That's because I had no idea how to get a party going, and I could be embarrassingly pretentious.

Back in the small kitchen I laid out on the worktop the peppers, the courgettes, the carrots, the garlic, the ginger and the bean sprouts and got ready to chop.

That's when the phone rang.

It was my aunt. She and my uncle had been over at my parents' house for Sunday lunch with my father and my grandmother who was living there at the time. By now my grandmother, that quietly implacable force who had held her family together through so much turmoil, was winding down from her life. She'd done it all. And then she'd done more. Because she had to. Because she loved her family. Because she was determined that they would succeed. At times when you were with her, her mind would slip off and head down paths you couldn't follow. And why not? So what if she would occasionally talk as if she'd spent the afternoon with her long-dead brothers? Maybe she wasn't losing her mind, maybe she was finding a different one. And if this different mind was vividly alive with people she had loved and lost, why was it necessarily such a bad thing?

My mother wasn't at the house. She'd flown to Singapore on Friday to take part in a storytelling festival. In all the years that my parents were married, it was one of the very few occasions they had been apart. That Sunday, everyone at the house had sat laughing and joking and eating round the circular table in the dining room. It was just one more happy meal to add to the countless others that had taken place there. At some point after the meal my aunt and uncle had gone off to Crystal Palace park to see a concert and would return later that night to say goodbye before heading home.

'You need to get to the hospital. It's your father.'

'What? What's happened? How is he?'

'You need to get to the hospital.'

I knew he was dead.

When people can't look you in the eye, you know there's no going back. It might be a lover you still love who's decided to leave you. It might be a boss who's decided he has to 'let you go'. It might be an aunt on a phone who can't bring herself to say the words. I know she was only trying to protect me from the worst. I know she was only hoping for the best. But we both knew that it was all too late.

'You need to get to the hospital.'

Seven words and the world turns upside down.

I didn't have a car. If I went by bus I would have to catch two of them and it would have taken too long. I didn't have any money for a taxi. I rang Steve, a friend from school. He came and picked me up and drove me to the hospital. I'd seen Steve just the day before. We'd been back at the school for an open day. We strolled around the grounds, soaked up the sunshine, watched a game of cricket, and laughed and joked with other schoolfriends in that easy way you have with people you grew up with. It was a beautiful afternoon.

I remember neon strip lights in a high and wide and busy hospital corridor. Harsh light. Unflattering light. Light no one looks good in because it reveals far too much. I spoke to someone at a desk and told them why I was there. I was taken away from the reception area, away from the high and wide corridor, where the life of the hospital pulsed, and shown into a smaller, quiet room. With soft lighting. With soft chairs.

At some point another family was shown into the room. I didn't catch their eye. They didn't catch mine. It was a very small room in which not to look at one another, but we managed it. Each, I suppose, lost and stumbling through a world that no longer made any sense.

A nurse came in and said that I could 'see the doctor now'. Another corridor, quieter, but still harsh neon lights. The doctor was young. He looked me in the eye. He had to. It was his job.

'I'm very sorry. But there was nothing we could do.'

I remember that when I looked into his eyes there was pain. He was upset. That has always stayed with me. I don't know what it means, but it means something. I hold on to it. For some reason it gives me hope.

'Would you like to see him?'

The doctor led me to a large white room with green screens dividing it roughly in two. We went behind the right-hand set of screens. My father was lying on some kind of table with a sheet covering most of his body. By the shapes under the sheet I could see that his shirt was undone and pulled back. His eyes were closed.

I took his hand in mine and held the strong fingers. The nails were still stained with nicotine from the cigarettes he'd long since given up. I ran my fingers over the hand I had known all my life. The hand that prepared the food. The hand that painted the paintings. The hand that stroked my hair when I was lying in bed drifting off to sleep.

But it was cold and that wasn't right. Why was it cold? Why didn't I feel it close around mine?

There were beads of sweat on my father's forehead. I pulled out a handkerchief from my pocket and gently wiped the sweat away.

I can't remember anything else. I don't want to remember anything else.

I walked from the hospital back to my parents' house. It was a long walk. But it wasn't far enough. If only I could go on walking forever then I'd never get home and if I never got home then I'd never have to meet my aunt and uncle who were waiting there, and if I never met my aunt and uncle then I'd never have to say the words, and if I never had to say the words then maybe the words wouldn't be true.

But I got home. Because there was nowhere else to go. And I said the words. Because there was nothing else to say.

Apparently, when my aunt and uncle had come back from the concert they found my father sitting at the round table. He had slumped forward and it looked like he was resting his head on his arms. My grandmother thought he had fallen asleep. Knowing that he'd worked hard getting all the food ready and then doing the washing up, she hadn't wanted to disturb him.

I sat by the phone for hours trying to ring my brother. He was away on business in the north of England. All I got was the answerphone on his mobile. It's not the kind of thing you can leave as a message.

Someone had already broken the news to my mother in Singapore, so when she rang me at least I didn't have to do that. Half a world away she asked if I was all right, told me that she was all right, and not to worry as she was getting the first flight back that she could. Despite the calmness of her voice I could hear the shock. Shock, and the knowledge that obviously there had been some kind of mistake.

I gave up trying to call my brother. I'd get him in the morning. I couldn't go to bed. I couldn't face being in the house. I put on my coat and went out of the front door and walked down to the park at the bottom of our road. I walked into the middle of the field where we used to play as kids. Games of football that lasted all day. Cricket with not enough fielders, so you soon got bored of chasing after the ball. Snowball fights that left you soaked to the skin and freezing and in line for a telling-off when you got home.

I sat in the middle of the field and waited for the sun to come up. I waited for the birds to start singing. I waited for the Routemasters to start ferrying people to work. I waited for my first day in this world without my father.

I got very cold.

Grief hollows out faces. Leaches out complexions. Dulls down hair. You look in the mirror and while you recognise who you see, you don't like who you see. You look at the people you love and you don't know what to do. Don't know what to say. And just as you don't know what to do or say, neither do those around you. Love helps. Love always helps. But it's not enough.

Absurd details take on huge significance. What kind of handles do you want on the coffin? How do you answer that one? Inside you're screaming I don't want any handles, I don't want a coffin, and I don't want my father to be dead. But outside you have to keep it all together. So you step back from the nightmare and try to consider the question rationally. And all the while you're being strong for everybody else. But all the while, all you really want to be is weak for yourself. To curl up on your bed and cry. To pull the covers over your head, shut out the world, drift off to sleep and wake to find that you're eight years old again and that it's the first day of the endless summer holidays and the sun is shining and it will never stop.

In the end you choose the simplest handles, consoling yourself with the thought that it is 'what he would have wanted'. But how do you know that?

I didn't see M again for years. No particular reason, it's just that our paths headed off in different directions. She'd stayed at the flat overnight and let herself out in the morning and gone home. The trout were never eaten. The sake was never drunk. I never opened the fortune cookies. Mind you, I did keep them for a long while. But then, I thought, if I did open them what could they possibly say to make any difference? Sometimes you don't need a fortune cookie to tell you the future.

But I have still got the handkerchief with which I mopped my father's brow. It's in an old Indian box I keep on a high shelf. Inside there's the handkerchief, my father's watch they gave me at the hospital, a cigar butt that he'd smoked that day, and a dried carnation. I suppose one day I'll throw them all out. But not yet. Not just yet.

The second most memorable meal I ever had, happened a few days before my father died. It was a meal to say good-bye to Mum before she set off for Singapore to go to the storytelling festival. It's only now that the irony of it all strikes me. We were saying goodbye to my mother, but it was my father we'd never see again.

As well as the farewell meal, my father had also completed the model of the house he was about to build in Cyprus. It must be any architect's dream to build their own house. And my father was on the verge of achieving the dream. When he showed me and my brother the model he was so happy. But what I remember most is that he really wanted us to like it. He wanted our approval. It was a gorgeous house that was to be built on the side of a gently sloping hill. It had a view of a lake, fruit trees all around and an ancient olive tree to be left growing in its place with the house tailored around its gnarled trunk.

That he wanted our approval I found incredibly moving. Why should what we think matter to him so much? Surely what he thought about us was what mattered? But all this was long before I had children of my own, so I didn't under-stand how beautiful and strange a thing it is to be a parent.

What we ate at that meal I have no idea. But it was the second most memorable meal I have ever had because it was the last time that I saw my father alive. It was the last time that my family was my family and we were all together. I try to remember more details of that night but they are gone, because at the time it was happening it was just another happy meal round the circular table in the dining room. I enjoyed the moment and let it go without even realising what I was losing.

twelve
and a half

A BRIEF HISTORY OF CURRY
IN BRITAIN: PART FOUR

Archduke Ferdinand was the next in line to take over the Austro-Hungarian Empire back at the start of the twentieth century. On the twenty-eighth of June 1914 he went to visit Sarajevo with his wife Sofia. It was, among other things, their wedding anniversary. The first gift they got on their journey to the town hall was a bomb thrown at them by a Serb nationalist. Luckily for them, but not for those behind, it bounced off the car and exploded next to the following vehicle. Despite the assassination attempt they carried on to the hall, the archduke made a speech, then they headed off on the shortest route out of the city. The most direct way out was mainly on a single straight road, but at one point the road almost turned back on itself. So at one point the motorcade would have to slow to a crawl. Unfortunately for Ferdy, another Serb was waiting at the turning point. With a gun. He shot two bullets. Sofia, who some say was pregnant, was killed instantly. Ferdinand died shortly after with his wife's name on his lips. The consequence of this was that, politically, all hell broke loose. All hell being the First World War.

When Britain got involved in the fight, many things in the country would end up changing irrevocably. The main change, of course, being the countless thousands of lives cut unnecessarily short. One of the smaller changes happened because the government was worried that as the working classes could buy alcohol at any time, then those employed as munitions workers might, if they'd been out on the piss the night before, not be in a fit state to churn out enough bullets and bombs come the morning. Their response was to bring in licensing laws. Alcohol could only be served between certain hours of the day.

These laws were still in place sixty or so years later in the 1970s when all the pubs would chuck out their customers at 11 p.m. The problem was that often these well-oiled drinkers would fancy 'jush one more'. Thanks to the idiosyncratic nature of the licensing laws, there was a way that they could quench their thirst. That's because, legally, you could go on drinking if your alcohol was served with a meal. But who would be willing to serve food to customers who were invariably, let's just say, a little worse for wear? Most established restaurants were closed or closing by the time the pubs shut. As they were established, they could afford to be choosy about who they served. The new Indian restaurants, however, were still struggling to make ends meet. In most cases they needed any custom they could get their hands on. So they stayed open and welcomed hordes of primarily thirsty customers who would stagger in from the pub. It is common lore in the Indian restaurant trade that most establishments in those days were only busy at two times – when the pubs chucked out after lunch, and at 11 p.m.

Of course, other people, in a less well-lubricated state, at other times were also eating in the Indian restaurants, but it was the post-pub session that firmly established an 'Indian' as part of the warp and weft of British popular culture. It was the true beginning of 'going for a curry' as something you did with your mates. And once people started going in just so that they could carry on drinking, they also discovered that a plateful of rice and curry had the added benefit of soaking up the beer. But, unfortunately, that's not all that was happening.

When I was eighteen, Brixton in South London exploded in riots. Primarily, it was a confrontation between disaffected black youth and a police force they saw as the heavy hand of a society that was increasingly rejecting them. (Others, of course, saw it as a chance to nick stuff and get away with it in the mayhem.) The coverage of events at the time made much of the fact that a lot of the trouble kicked off in a street called Railton Road, which was dubbed the 'front line'.

Well, if Railton Road was the front line between certain sections of black and white society in the 1970s and 1980s, then I'd argue that the front line between certain sections of Asian and white society was the Taj Mahal, or the Koh-I-Noor, or the Bombay Palace or any one of countless other Indian restaurants at chucking-out time on a Friday or Saturday night. And though these particular front lines never erupted into riots, they did, all too often, descend into endless low-level racist skirmishes.

While, no doubt, the majority of the people who abused the waiters who served them only saw it as a bit of a laugh, the context, especially in the 1970s, held something far darker in its shadows. Whereas the black community was often seen as one that would fight back, the Asian community was seen as a soft option. 'Paki-bashing' occasionally went a lot further. After one particular racist murder, the then leader of the National Front greeted the news with the words, 'One down, a million to go.'

Thankfully, somewhere along the line, things started to change. Perhaps it was the very extremism of the violent fascists that acted as a wake-up call to others, who realised that maybe while calling a waiter 'Gunga Din' was 'just a bit of fun', it did, in fact, sit at one end of a continuum that at the other end had hate-fuelled violence. Maybe the more people that ate in Indian restaurants and started to see them as a place where you had a good time with your mates, the harder it was to accept a characterisation of Asians based on either ridicule or demonisation. Or maybe the food was just so damned enjoyable that the taint of prejudice was washed away with pleasure.

And speaking of washing things away with pleasure,

why is lager the drink of choice with a curry? I mean, it's not as if it's a particularly Asian beverage. Back in the days of the Raj, if the British drank beer it would have been beer, not lager. IPA, for instance, stands for India Pale Ale – a brew specifically concocted with an excess of hops that helped preserve it on the long journey out to the subcontinent. The most commonly expounded explanation is that when the King of Denmark frequented the upmarket Veeraswamy's, he insisted on being able to drink a pint or two of home brew. The home brew in his case being Carlsberg. From that moment on, apparently, curry and lager went together like peaches and cream. Whether the story is true is debatable. It was recently claimed to have been made up by an inventive marketing man.

To my mind, the likelier explanation is much more prosaic. In the 1960s and early 1970s British breweries didn't make much, if any, lager. And the majority of pubs were tied to a brewery. So when European lager-makers decided to crack the British market they found getting distribution in pubs very difficult. Getting into most restaurants was also a non-starter because restaurants primarily served wine. But they could get distribution through Indian restaurants. And these were establishments whose potential the British brewers were very slow to recognise. So the lager-makers got a market, and the Indian restaurant owners got the alcohol they needed to tempt in the post-pub crowd. And the customers were able to do the very simple mental calculation:

Hot curry + cold lager = No longer burning mouth

In a sense, which version of events is true doesn't really matter as myths and legends have always been an integral part of the rise of curry in Britain. For example, the ubiquitous chicken tikka masala is reputed to have originated when a customer in an Indian restaurant sent his chicken tikka back to the kitchen because it was 'too dry'. The chef, at a loss how to address the complaint, spied a tin of Campbell's tomato soup on a shelf and added it, with a few spices, to the meat, and a national bestseller was born. Now although a fair few restaurants claim to be the one where this incident took place, no one can verify the story, let alone adjudicate on the competing claims.

Likewise the recent baltification of Birmingham. Many restaurants based in the city proudly declare that it was on their premises that balti was first cooked. But even the origin of the word is open to dispute. Some say it lies in the fact that *balti* is a Hindi word for bucket, and hence the name of the style of cooking is based on the large bowls in which the food was served. Others say the word's roots lie in the Pakistani Himalayan province of Baltistan.

Of course, the biggest myth about curry is that in the 1970s it would invariably give the clientele who staggered in after a night in the pub a decidedly dodgy tummy the morning after. Apparently the 112 pints of lager they'd downed before collapsing into a chair and demanding the hottest vindaloo on earth had nothing whatsoever to do with it. (Neither did the fact that they always ate too much curry with too little rice.)

But talking of the Ring of Fire machismo of demanding

the hottest thing on the menu brings us to possibly one of the key moments in the absorption and acceptance of curry into the cultural body of Britain. It came when the predominantly Asian cast of *Goodness Gracious Me* unleashed the 'Going For An English' sketch on the British public. It took the cliché of a bunch of inebriated lads and ladettes rounding off their evening by 'going for an Indian' and turned it on its head. In the sketch a group of raucous Indians, in India, finish off their night by 'going for an English' and demanding 'the blandest thing on the menu'. It was a very clever and very funny piece of work. What lifted it into something far more significant was the response to it. Asian audiences loved it because it subverted the stereotypes and poked fun at the majority white population. But the white population watched it, recognised the parody of their own absurdities and foibles, and fell about laughing too. And if there is one thing that brings people together more than anything else in the world, it is the ability to laugh. If we share a sense of humour, then how different can we be?

But back to the story of curry itself. The rise of the takeaway was another key factor in curry's infiltration of the mainstream. The advantage for the restaurateurs was that it enabled them to sell to customers who didn't want the full-on (and often 'lively') Indian restaurant experience. For the customers it was also usually cheaper as they didn't feel obliged to order relatively expensive alcohol, or they could get the drinks in from the off-licence. And they could eat while watching the telly. What also worked in the takeaway's favour was that lifestyles were changing. People cooked at home less frequently, they lived in more single-person households, and the rise of the long-hours work culture meant workers arrived home of an evening too knackered to cook and feeling that they'd 'earned' a curry.

The other advantage curry has is, of course, that it's the perfect takeaway food. Pizzas go cold and if you reheat them in the oven they dry out, or go soggy in the microwave. Fish and chips are best eaten when still crisp and hot and, anyway, can seem too ordinary. And Chinese food, mainly based on stir-frying, is best served and eaten straight from the wok. Curries, however, being essentially spicy stews, both travel well and don't suffer when reheated. So having a takeaway curry is pretty much the same eating experience as one you get when you sit down in an Indian restaurant.

But as long ago as the 1960s, the takeaway wasn't the only way to get a curry at home.

In terms of the narrative of this book, three important things happened in 1962. First, and obviously most crucially, I was born. Then the government passed the Commonwealth Immigration Act, limiting the number of migrants coming to Britain – which strikes me as a bit of an overreaction. Then a company called Vesta was launched.

Vesta was at the very cutting edge of food technology. In a time when the world was riveted by the space race between the United States and the Soviet Union, Vesta had their own 'one small step for man, one giant leap for mankind' moment, by realising that the real benefit to humanity to come out of the billions spent on conquering the infinite void that lay above earth's skies would be in the ready meal market. They grabbed the technique by which the astronauts' food was dehydrated and ran with it all the way to the supermarket. First up was Vesta Chicken Curry. Then they upped the technology ante by launching a 'beef' curry made with processed soya shaped into little meat-like chunks. Despite the fact that they tasted dire, they were a big success. Maybe it was the glamour of the space race rubbing off. Or maybe Vesta's masterstroke was the fact that they launched a curry product aimed at a market that was still relatively uninformed as to what a curry should really taste like.

(Incidentally, it's recently come to light that John Lennon's favourite meal when he was married to Cynthia was Vesta beef curry with banana sliced into it. So maybe when he set off to India to search of enlightenment, all he really wanted to become one with was a decent curry.)

While Vesta's success with dehydrated food may now seem little more than a lay-by just off the motorway that is curry in Britain, it does reveal one of the key recurring themes. Namely, curry's affinity with technological advances. Ready-made curry sauces were the result of a process started, allegedly, by L.G. Pathak (the founding father of the all-conquering Patak brand). His aim was to find a way to make curry spices taste better and, more importantly, last longer. The main problem being that in the 1970s and 1980s when people tried to make curries at home, they would never use freshly ground spices but ones that had been sitting around on shelves for ages and so had lost a lot of the subtleties of their original flavours. Mr

Pathak's solution was to blend the relevant roasted and ground spices for a particular curry, then mix them with oil. From there it was but a small step to the creamier cook-in sauces that dominate the market today.

All of which brings me back to my Road To Damascus moment in aisle seven of the Harringey branch of Sainsbury's back at the start of this book. But the man I blame for my falling from the culinary grace of my heritage isn't Mr Pathak. Oh no. It's a certain Mr Noon. Mr, now Sir, G.K. Noon.

It all began with Mr Noon's grandfather who started a sweetshop in Bombay in 1898. Over the years the business prospered, but by the time G.K. had a hand in the decision-making he wanted to step up a gear. In 1962, as an early indicator of his willingness to innovate to grow his company, he installed air-conditioning in the shop. At the time this would have been very expensive and unheard-of in most retail establishments. But the gamble paid off. Customers flocked into the new premises, which he had also completely restyled. His next step was to halt sweet production at the shop and invest in a factory. This too was a success and before long the company – Royal Sweets – was a firmly established high-flyer. The financial rewards that accrued meant that the one-time sweet-seller was soon expanding into other areas, such as paper, print and construction.

In 1970, always on the lookout for fresh fields and pastures new, Mr Noon turned to Southall in London. By 1973 his newly opened shop wasn't just selling products he imported from India, but making them too. World politics had also stepped in to play a hand. Surprisingly, the dealer of the hand in question had no time for Asians. He was Idi Amin, President – or should that be emperor? – of Uganda. In 1972 he kicked all the Asians out of his country. Many arrived in Britain with next to nothing. That subsequently so many of them have done so well in this country is a testament to both their resilience and their drive. And while they may have arrived with little more than the clothes they stood up in, they did bring with them a taste for Indian food. And Indian sweets. And Mr Noon was there offering, so to speak, the rasmalais of comfort.

Next stop for Mr Noon was New York, where he joined forces with the Taj Group of Hotels and opened up a factory producing chilled and frozen Indian food. Unfortunately, America, despite being part of the continent that first sent the chilli over to India, was not ready to welcome back the culinary results of that horticultural transplantation. Like so many of the finer cultural things in life, the Americans just didn't get curry. But back in Britain, Mr Noon realised that the obviously far more discerning public not only 'got' curry, but, increasingly, couldn't get enough of it. And the market that was booming the most was the supermarket ready meal. Mainly this was because the British love affair with curry was starting to hit its stride. But also it was because the food manufacturers had discovered that the curry was a meal whose production could be easily, and successfully, mechanised with relatively little loss of quality.

The only problem was, as Mr Noon clearly understood, that it's no good if you have a production process that doesn't degrade the quality of the food it produces, if the recipes you start off with are decidedly naff. And that's the state of affairs that confronted G.K. in Britain. All of which led him to the conclusion of a born entrepreneur: I can do better. And he did. First he convinced Birds Eye to let him take over production of their frozen curries. Next up it was British Airways. And then in 1989 he landed the big one: Sainsbury's.

The gap in the market that he targeted was the British consumer who wanted to eat authentic curry but didn't have the time, or the knowledge, to make it for themselves. That this British consumer might one day include a second-generation Asian immigrant like myself is a turn of events that I doubt he would have predicted.

And seeing as my encounter with a jar of Sainsbury's own label korma sauce is where this whole story kicked off, it seems a most appropriate place to end this Brief History of Curry in Britain.

thirteen

THE WINE WILL BE FLAT

William Makepeace Thackeray, a contemporary and rival of Charles Dickens, is most famous for writing *Vanity Fair*. What's less well known about him is that he was Indian. I base this somewhat surprising (and misleading) assertion on the fact that he was born in Calcutta in 1811. He was the son of Richard Thackeray – a collector for the East India Company, who himself may well have been the descendant of an Anglo-Indian liaison somewhere up the line. Mr Thackeray senior died in 1815, which resulted in his four-year-old son being sent 'back' to England to be educated.

But obviously his Indian childhood had left a lasting impression on him as in 1846 he wrote, and had published, the following poem:

Curry
Three pounds of veal my darling girl prepares,

And chops it nicely into little squares
Five onions next prures the little minx
(The biggest are the best, her Samiwel thinks),
And Epping butter nearly half a pound,
And stews them in a pan until they're brown'd.
What's next my dextrous little girl will do?
She pops the meat into the savoury stew,
With curry-powder table-spoonfuls three,
And milk a pint (the richest that may be).
And, when the dish has stewed for half an hour,
A lemon's ready juice she'll o'er it pour.
Then, bless her! Then she gives the luscious pot
A very gentle boil – and serves quite hot.
P.S. – Beef, mutton, rabbit if you wish,
Lobsters, or prawns, or any kind of fish,
Are fit to make a CURRY. 'Tis, when done,
A dish for Emperors to feed upon.

While the poem did not strike as immediate a chord with the British public as *Vanity Fair* did, the very fact that he both wrote it, and included it in a collection called *Kitchen Melodies*, clearly shows that while curry might well have been decidedly exotic back then, it was most definitely not unheard of.

Incidentally, reread the poem and you can't help but suspect that it wasn't only the prospect of the impending curry that was raising William's temperature. After all, the cook in the poem is first referred to as 'my darling girl', next as a 'little minx', and then you get the following couplet:

What's next my dextrous little girl will do?
She pops the meat into the savoury stew,

Now it could just be me, and the fact that I've been watching too much Graham Norton, but I can't help thinking there is a very strong sexual subtext sloshing about in the nether regions of the poem. I mean, just imagine Leslie Phillips, with a twinkle in his eye and wry grin on his lips, reciting the thing. So, while on the surface it might appear to be a poem about the delights of curry, I put it to you that it is in fact a coded homily to the reputed aphrodisiac powers of the dish.

All of which leads me, fairly obviously, to Paul Weller, the Jam and the classic 1978 song 'Down In A Tube Station At Midnight'.

Down In A Tube Station At Midnight
The distant echo –
Of faraway voices boarding faraway trains
To take them home to
The ones that they love and who love them forever
The glazed, dirty steps – repeat my own and reflect
* my thoughts*
Cold and uninviting, partially naked
Except for toffee wrappers and this morning's paper
Mr Jones got run down
Headlines of death and sorrow – they tell of tomorrow
Madmen on the rampage
And I'm down in the tube station at midnight
I fumble for change – and pull out a queen

Smiling beguiling
I put in the money and pull out a plum
Behind me
Whispers in the shadows – gruff blazing voices
Hating, waiting
Hey boy they shout – have you got any money?
And I said – I've a little money and a takeaway
  curry,
I'm on my way home to my wife
She'll be lining up the cutlery
You know she's expecting me
Polishing the glasses and pulling out the cork
And I'm down in a tube station at midnight

The song goes on:

I first felt a fist, and then a kick
I could now smell their breath
They smelt of pubs and Wormwood Scrubs
And too many right-wing meetings

The song ends with the narrator lying in a heap on the floor of the tube station lamenting his fate with the line:

The wine will be flat and the curry's gone cold
Don't wanna go down in a tube station at midnight

To most people it's not really a song about curry. For them, and most of the time for me, it's a brilliantly imagined vignette of 1970s suburban life, given a pulse-quickening drive by Bruce Foxton's killer bass line and Paul Weller's clipped and angry vocals. But I'd argue it is precisely because it is not about curry that the song is, profoundly, about curry. And curry's acceptance as part of the urban, working-class, British way of life. The hero of the song is just going about his normal, everyday life. Taking a curry home after work is just another unremarkable part of his unremarkable day.

Also, writers don't choose words by accident. In 1978, in Britain, the National Front was on the rise. Paul Weller's narrator is jumped by lagered-up louts who'd been to 'too many right-wing meetings'. But the narrator was carrying home a curry. Now I don't think it is too far-fetched to suggest that down in that tube station at midnight, two competing views of the possible future of Britain were clashing in a four-minute pop song.

Twenty years after the Jam stormed the charts, and 152 years after William Makepeace was waxing lyrical, curry once again made an appearance in popular culture. Read the following extract from the work of art in question and you may well be tempted to conclude that the emphasis was more on 'popular' than 'culture'.

It all took place during the 1998 World Cup finals in France. And followed in an age-old tradition that goes all the way back to the Golden Era of the Mexico tournament in 1970, when the nation's airwaves were awash with the silken tones of Moore, Banks, Peters and the rock god that was Bobby Charlton serenading us with 'Back Home'.

(Unfortunately, the song's title was just a touch too prophetic as England got knocked out in the quarter-finals by Germany after they'd been two–nil up. Bloody Peter Bonetti.)

Yes, we are dancing, Nobby Stiles-like, on the hallowed turf that is the England football team song. After 'Back Home', the next ditty of any note was New Order's 'World In Motion' with M.C. Barnesy's era-defining rap which, when it crossed the pond, obviously inspired a juvenile Eminem to quit the church choir and start wearing his base-ball cap back to front.

Then we get the Lightning Seeded magic of Skinner and Baddiel's 'Three Lions' – a song that so embedded itself in the nation's consciousness that it directly led to the removal of the Tory Party from government after eighteen years in power. This, I know, is a large and somewhat controversial claim, but I back it up with the following extract from a speech given by Tony Blair to the Labour Party conference only a few months before the 1997 election that swept him into power:

I don't care where you're coming from; it's where your country's going that matters. If you believe in what I believe in, join the team. Labour has come home to you. So come home to us. Labour's coming home. Seventeen years of hurt. Never stopped us dreaming. Labour's coming home. As we did in 1945. I know that was then, but it could be again. Labour's coming home.

God, did we really fall for such nonsense? Well, apparently we did. Three times. But with the benefit of hindsight, maybe Mr Blair's choice of metaphor was prophetic in a way that he couldn't possibly have guessed at the time. After all, don't England's football campaigns all tend to go the same way? Incredibly high hopes at the start, always ending in disillusionment and disappointment. (And the search for a new manager.)

Anyway, you can see how the England football team song can play a pivotal role in the nation's social, cultural and, indeed, political life. It also provides, via the vehicle of a song about the national sport's national team, an opportunity for an artistic examination and celebration of national identity.

All of which brings us to this:

Vindaloo

Where on earth are you from?
We're from England
Where you come from
Do you put the kettle on?
Kick it
Nah nah nah
Nah nah nah
Nah nah nah
Nah nah nah nah nah
Nah nah nah
Bon jour
Nah nah nah

Monsieur
Nah nah nah
Nah nah nah nah nah
Nah nah nah
Nah nah nah
Nah nah nah
Nah nah nah nah
We're England
We're gonna score one more than you
England!
Can I introduce you please
To a lump of Cheddar cheese
Knit one, Pearl one
Drop one, Curl one
Kick it
Nah nah nah
Nah nah nah
Nah nah nah
Nah nah nah nah nah
Nah nah nah
Nah nah nah
Nah nah nah
Nah nah nah nah nah
Nah nah nah
Nah nah nah
Nah nah nah
Nah nah nah nah
We're from England
We're gonna score one more than you

England!
Me and me Mum and me Dad and me Gran
We're off to Waterloo
Me and me Mum and me Dad and me Gran
And a bucket of Vindaloo
Bucket!
Vindaloo
Vindaloo
Vindaloo
Vindaloo
Vindaloo nah nah
Vindaloo
Vindaloo
And we all like Vindaloo
We're England
We're gonna score one more than you
England!
Nah nah nah
Vindaloo
Nah nah nah
Nah nah nah nah nah
Nah nah nah
Vindaloo
Nah nah nah
Vindaloo
Nah nah nah
Nah nah nah nah nah
Vindaloo
Vindaloo

> *And we all like Vindaloo*
> *We're England*
> *We're gonna score one more than you*
> *England!*

Well, who wouldn't be moved?

Much has been said and written about the dumbing-down of contemporary Britain but I think this magnum opus (which is Latin for big opus, or, maybe, an opus-flavoured ice cream) clearly lays that particular canard to rest.

It is a work of genius.

While on the face of it this literary gem might not seem to be a worthy addition to the canon of English works that includes the likes of Chaucer, Wordsworth, Shelley and Byron, I would argue that it, in fact, draws inspiration from, and reinterprets for a modern audience, some of the greatest words of our greatest artist.

Just consider the following:

> *Now all the youth of England are on fire,*
> *And silken dalliance in the wardrobe lies;*
> *Now thrive the armourers, and honour's thought*
> *Reigns solely in the breast of every man:*

And:

> *We few, we happy few, we band of brothers;*
> *For he to-day that sheds his blood with me*
> *Shall be my brother; be he ne'er so vile*

This day shall gentle his condition:
And gentlemen in England, now a-bed
Shall think themselves accurs'd they were not here,
And hold their manhoods cheap whiles any speaks
That fought with us upon Saint Crispin's day.

And:

I see you stand like greyhounds in the slips,
Straining upon the start. The game's afoot:
Follow your spirit; and upon this charge
Cry 'God for Harry, England and Saint George!'

Well, let's be honest here. What is 'We're gonna score one more than you' but a contemporary reimagining of Shakespeare's stirring call to arms, 'Cry "God for Harry, England and Saint George!"'

And should you remain unconvinced as to the relevance of the Bard's work to that of Fat Les, just consider this. Henry the Fifth was rallying the troops to do battle against France. And where were the 1998 World Cup finals being held? That's right, in France.

What's remarkable about the song, in terms of this book, is that it positions a curry at the very centre of a hymn to national identity and national pride. Now, how likely would that have been even ten years earlier?

And go back ten years before that, and what do you think Paul Weller's reaction would have been had he realised there'd be a fair chance that the same right-wing thugs who beat up his everyday hero down in the tube station (at midnight) would be on the Continent badge-kissingly bellowing their Englishness with a song called 'Vindaloo'?

And what about William Makepeace Thackeray? What would he make of it all? Well, actually, he'd probably get the joke. That's because he was a razor-sharp satirical observer. And you just know that anyone who used pseudonyms like George Savage Fitz-Boodle, C.J. Yellowplush Esq., and Michael Angelo Titmarsh had a decent sense of humour.

So the Fat Les song was as much satirising an idea of Englishness as celebrating it. And vindaloo, for so long the butt (and I use that word advisedly) of generations of frankly racist jokes (yes, I am looking at you, Mr Davidson), was here being used affectionately. It was as English as knitting, Cheddar cheese and putting the kettle on. And something that your mum, your dad and even your gran could safely down by the bucketload.

I recently asked my mother why it was that all the time I was growing up we would traditionally eat our version of vindaloo with chunks of fresh white bread at about half one in the morning, after coming back from midnight mass on Christmas Eve. After all, delicious though it is, by no stretch of the imagination could it ever be described as a particularly light curry.

My mother's answer took me back with her to Christmas 1941 in Burma, the day after the Japanese had first bombed Rangoon. Although the first bombing raid had been on the twenty-third of December, things had been slowly starting to malfunction for quite some time before. If order hadn't actually collapsed, it was looking decidedly shaky. My mother's family tried to carry on as normal as best they could, but in order to avoid the bombs they had moved out of the city and were lodging in a village not far away. Despite the interruption, midnight mass was an unbreakable appointment that everyone in the family would be woken up to attend.

The children were roused from their beds, dressed in their best clothes, then they would join the adults on the walk to the church. En route, a quiet excitement would fill the warm, still air. That's because after midnight mass the next stop would be Christmas Day itself. And Christmas Day would be the day when you could eat more than was sensible and finally, finally get to open your presents.

The service itself on Christmas Eve was long. The priest would drone on in Latin and the packed congregation would speak the responses with one voice. Hymns and carols would be sung out loud with baritone voices flying low over the pews, while sopranos would swoop and circle with the harmonies. The sermon, when it came, would inevitably concern itself with the true meaning of Christmas.

With war in the air and the threat of the Japanese drawing ever closer, Christmas 1941 felt more precious than ever. No one knew what the months ahead would hold, but this moment, this celebration, this gathering of a community for maybe the last time, this Christmas, was special.

Every second somehow defiantly declared this is who we are, this is what we believe, this is how we live. And in the morning there would be presents.

At last the service was over and everyone slowly, and happily, left the church. Hands were shaken, laughter was heard, and Christmas wishes exchanged as, reluctantly, everyone took their leave and headed home.

Halfway home a delicious aroma filled the air. It was bread. Freshly baked bread. Bread which, because of the disruption of the last couple of weeks, couldn't be had for love nor money. My grandfather turned to his family and said that they should track down the bakery now because who knows when they'd be able to get fresh bread again. So they did. And they bought loaf after loaf of freshly baked, crusty, piping hot white bread.

When he eventually got his brood back home, the aroma of the bread had become too irresistible. So an executive decision was taken to eat the bread there and then. But what to have with it? That was the question. My grandmother went into the kitchen and saw the large pot of vindaloo that was to be one of the centrepieces of the lunch in ten hours' time. Oh well, there'd be plenty left over. It's not as if there wasn't lots of other food to eat.

That's why every Christmas, all the time that I was growing up, my family would eat vindaloo scooped up with fresh, white, crusty bread at half one in the morning of Christmas Day after a trip to midnight mass. For me it is, along with Slade and tank-tops and 'Will I get a Rubik's cube?', a quintessential memory of 1970s Christmases. For my mother it is a memory of a last Christmas in Burma before the world turned upside down.

VINDALOO

SERVES 8

2kg pork, cut into large cubes
4 tablespoons vinegar, plus more if required
salt
4 large onions, finely sliced
6 tablespoons vegetable oil
2 teaspoons chilli powder, 2 teaspoons turmeric,
    4 teaspoons ginger paste, 4 teaspoons garlic paste,
    2 teaspoons cumin powder, 2 teaspoons mustard
    powder, 4 teaspoons coriander powder, made into
    a paste
1 teaspoon sugar
4 large tomatoes, sliced
1 teaspoon paprika

Wash the pork then soak overnight in 4 tablespoons of vinegar and a teaspoon of salt.

Fry the onions in the oil. Add the spice paste and cook gently for 3 minutes – don't burn. Add a little water gradually, and sugar, tomatoes and paprika. When the oil comes to the top of the mixture, add the drained pork. Stir well. Simmer over a low heat until the pork is tender and the gravy thickens. Add more vinegar, sugar and salt as required. Tends to taste best 1–2 days after cooking.

fourteen
LENTILS, LENTILS EVERYWHERE

When I went to university I discovered whole new dimensions to curry. Both in my first year in a hall of residence and also in the two years after I moved out.

The hall of residence in question was St George's Hall at Reading University. I was studying Human Geography. The course lasted three years. I got a 2:1. But even back then I would find it hard, come the inevitable Christmas-at-home cross-examination by uncles and aunts, to describe what the course was actually about. It had politics in it, it had economics in it, it had sociology in it. It even had a little bit of geography in it. I found it, at the time, incredibly interesting, but on graduating discovered that in terms of getting a job it was easily in the top ten of most useless degrees. This was back in the early 1980s when useless degrees hadn't really burgeoned into the boom sector that it is now.

St George's Hall was the least hip hall of residence at Reading. And Reading itself wasn't exactly awash with excitements. I think I'm right in saying that at the time the town had one nightclub – the aptly named Target – that was housed in a bunker alongside the Butts Shopping Centre and which students were warned off for fear of being beaten up. As a result, for most students social life revolved around the campus.

Having said all this, the moment the taxi from the station deposited me into the drive of St George's Hall I was filled with what I took to be an incredibly grown-up sense of excitement. I looked up at the five-storey, 1970s block of flats that made up the bulk of the place and thought, somewhat hopefully, so this is where I'm really going to start living. I was allocated a room on the third floor with a window that looked out towards a road, a line of trees and a glimpse of the playing fields at the edge of the campus.

Food was included in the price of the room. I was going to say that food was thrown in, but that would have been too obvious a line. It's not that the food was bad, it was just that it was typical mass catering of the time. It had been cooked in bulk in a large kitchen. It was eaten in bulk in a large hall. And the menu was set in a weekly rotation – if it's Monday it must be chicken – that seldom varied. Occasionally, a curry would make an appearance. But mass-catering curry hadn't really moved on much from my first encounter with one in the 1970s.

The vast majority of students at Reading were white. The only black or brown faces you saw would be overseas

264

students. Much to my shame I never really made the effort to get to know any of the students from abroad, and as I wasn't alone in this, they tended to socialise mainly with others from overseas. But it's not as if I wasn't encountering other cultures. After all, I had lived in London all my life, so meeting Geordies and Scots and people whose parents were farmers, and others from towns and cities across the country was enough of a sociological eye-opener. I distinctly remember wondering why all of them were so friendly. I mean, what were they after? It wasn't until much later that I figured out what was going on. They weren't after anything – they just weren't from London.

Had I made the effort to get to know any of the overseas students I would have discovered that, in fact, there was good food at university. It was being cooked by the foreign students.

At St George's Hall all meals were provided except for Sunday evening. Then you were left to fend for yourself. For most of the inmates this meant tea and toast and the ubiquitous Marmite. Or maybe the heady heights of a tin of beans cooked on the Baby Belling that sat in the cleaning-cupboard of a kitchen each corridor had, charmingly positioned next to the communal bathroom and toilets.

There was, however, one among us who cooked a proper meal every Sunday night. His name I have long since forgotten but I can clearly see him, a somewhat pale, bulky and bespectacled figure, hunched over a bubbling pan while all around him were the strewn ingredients of whatever he was cooking. And it was usually a curry. A curry that had to be constantly stirred and fiddled with and tasted. All of which, along with his lank straggly hair and shuffling gait, gave him the demeanour of some otherworldly shaman muttering incantations from a gravy-stained book of spells, while tending to a cauldron of mysteries. The fact that he was a big fan of Saxon and Marillion and had three-foot-high speakers for the stereo in his room also marked him out as somewhat of a loner. He was, of course, studying computers. And rereading *The Lord of The Rings*.

The curry thing intrigued me, however. There was something about the fact that it needed so many ingredients, that it took so long to cook, that it required constant nurturing and that it was foreign, that gave it a weird intangible power. It was yet another way that this head-banging, microchipped, orc-speaking geek had chosen to define his otherness. Curry was a mystery you had to be initiated into. It was a threshold that only the fortunate few had crossed. And he was one of the chosen.

Most odd.

The other thing I remember about those long, dull, Sunday evenings is walking down the corridors of St George's and hearing Alan Freeman's rocktastic voice running down the Top Thirty on every single radio, in every single room. As it was a time when pop, rock, soul, punk, reggae, disco, new wave, Two Tone and new romantic records could all make their way into the Top Ten, keeping tabs on who was where in the charts was vital if you wanted to maintain your cred down at the jukebox in the student union bar.

The other revelation about curry, however, only happened after I moved out of the hall of residence.

When you move out, you move into a whole new world. You're no longer paddling in the shallow end of independence, but thrown head first into the sea.

You have to find a place to live, and people to share with, and buy your own food, and cook your own food, and keep the place clean, and not piss off the neighbours, and not piss off your housemates, and learn not to get pissed off by them, and also get a grip on that most shocking of revelations – that if you use electricity or gas or the phone, you have to pay the bills. Then there's the rent. And the landlords who made Rigsby look like a philanthropist.

Hanging out in student houses with people who have to cook their food for themselves also brings you face to fork with that veritable Che Guevara poster of student cuisine – the Vegetable Curry.

If, for our friend in the hall-of-residence kitchen, slaving over a bubbling pot of curry was somehow personal, here in the shapeless form of vegetable curry it was most definitely political.

This was the time of the miners' strike, anti-apartheid marches and the Greenham Common women. Every other week it seemed that there would be notices up in the student union telling us what time the coaches would be leaving that Saturday to ferry protesters to London, to protest about things that obviously needed to be vociferously protested about. And if parading through the capital behind a home-made banner, while a lone voice endlessly shouted, 'Thatcher! Thatcher! Thatcher!' and we endlessly replied, 'Out! Out! Out!', was politics writ large in the public sphere, then private conflicts were often waged across the battlefield of what you dished up for your dinner.

The prevailing attitude was eloquently summed up on a badge of the time: 'Meat Is Murder'. Obviously I didn't go along with such nonsense. Although I could see the logic of what the radical evangelical vegetarians were saying, given my fondness for my mother's cooking I always came back to the thought: but meat tastes really nice. I had even been known, after a night drinking cider at the student union, to wolf down a burger of dubious provenance from Greasy Joe's burger van, which held an all-night vigil outside the front gates of the campus. All of which meant that in terms of 'right on-ness' I was most definitely a straggler at the back of the march, more interested in chatting to his mates than bringing the government down.

However, I did frequently bump into people who were big beasts in the whole vegetarian scene. Back then vegetarian food seemed to consist entirely of lentils, chickpeas, cheese, eggs and vegetable bakes that were as tough as rhino hide. (On second thoughts, given that we're in the land of radical vegetarians here, maybe rhino hide isn't the most appropriate analogy.)

There was also vegetable curry. Everyone you met had a recipe for vegetable curry. Unfortunately everyone had the same recipe and it was awful. It consisted of whatever bruised and battered vegetables had been going cheap down at the market just before it closed, a teaspoon of jaded

curry powder, a clove of garlic, and a tin of chopped tomatoes chucked over the top to give it some gravy. Then the
whole affair was simmered into sludgedom while a 'house
meeting' went on to debate for two hours whether the fact
that the boys never cleaned the bath was just another
expression of 'de facto dictatorial and paternalistic oppres-
sion of women'.

The conclusion I came to when I unenthusiastically
partook of a plateful was that in order to be a vegetarian,
you had to have your taste buds removed. And, in truth, I
was only eating it because I fancied the girl who cooked it.
Obviously, I got nowhere with her. I mean, the very fact
that I thought of her as a 'girl' shows I was too far from
understanding the fundamental issues of feminism ever to
stand a chance.

It's only looking back that I can figure out what the
student vegetable curry was all about. It wasn't about food.
It was a political statement. It was a badge of belonging for
those who rejected the prevailing order. It was a secret sign
with as much history and hidden meaning and power as a
Masonic handshake.

Unfortunately, it tasted so appalling that it could put
you off curried vegetables for life.

It was while I was at university that I first went to an Indian
restaurant. This might seem rather late in the day, but while
I was living at home what would have been the point? At
my parents' place I would get fantastic Indian food every

week. If we were to go to a restaurant, why would we choose an Indian one? The food wouldn't have been as good, it would have cost three times as much, and you'd have to share the dining experience with a room full of people you didn't know.

It's not as if we went out to eat at restaurants that often. Or, indeed, at all. If I wrack my brains I think I can just about remember the occasional family meal at a Chinese restaurant. As an eighteen-year-old schoolboy, flushed with his Saturday earnings from selling furniture in the Camberwell branch of MFI, I think I also took my girl-friend out for dinner at a Berni Inn. We even drank wine – which made us feel the height of sophistication. What I'm driving at is that eating out was not a part of my everyday vocabulary. So the fact that by the time I reached university I had never eaten at an Indian restaurant is not surprising.

The restaurant was up a steep flight of stairs on a side road off Reading's high street. Inside it was large and airy and as flock-wallpapered as you could wish for. By now I was going out with a girl who was studying to be a teacher and who, handily, lived in the house next door to ours. We chose the restaurant because we'd not fancied any of the other ones we'd walked past that evening. The fact that it was an Indian restaurant was not something I had given much thought to until the moment I opened the menu. That my date was scanning the menu unsure what to order was to be expected. That I was in the same position was less so. But the truth was that I recognised very little of what was on the menu. At home a chicken curry was a chicken curry.

Different types of curry were described by the ingredients that went into them. So I'd grown up with curries that didn't have names. Staring down the menu, I realised that I didn't know my madras from my dopiaza. As I looked across the table, the girl I was still trying to impress closed her menu and said, 'You know about this, why don't you order?'

In the end we had a chicken korma and a biriani. They were the only two main courses I recognised. And I must have done something right because we were together for the next couple of years.

fifteen

PLASTIC BOXES

My father was a good cook. But he didn't cook that often. The cooking was mainly done by my mother. I'm sure my father would have liked to cook more, but he was the one who went out to work all day so, as a matter of practicality, it was easier if my mother did the cooking. When my mother started teaching full-time in a primary school, things didn't change because the school day finished at half three, so she would still get home a full three hours before my father did.

The primary school my mother taught at was just up the road. It was typical of many inner London primaries of the time. It was housed in the old, battered, high-waisted Victorian buildings that were so solid they'd outlasted two world wars and the fall of an empire.

Corridors stretched for miles and echoed to small feet that were constantly straining not to break into a run. Light shafted across rooms from tall windows divided into square panes. And playgrounds were places walled-in and hard-surfaced where half the time you played, and half the time you survived.

But while the structure of the place had remained unchanged for generations, the contents definitely hadn't. It was still a local school, for local people, but now the local people hailed from some very exotic places. Look around the playground and while white faces were still in the major-ity, there were now a growing number of brown ones. And black ones. And Greek ones. And Chinese ones.

All this was back in the 1970s. In those days, multicul-turalism was hardly ever seen as a positive thing. Indeed, the very word 'multiculturalism' was rarely used. A plurality of races was not seen as a situation that had anything to offer within a school. Instead, it was seen as a problem that had to be managed.

Of course, a debate on the subject did exist within the teaching profession, but the ones who saw and argued for the possible benefits of having children from different worlds in the same school were not in the majority. The other problem was that teaching is probably the most full-on job there is. Faced with a class of thirty demanding children every single day, it is hard for any teacher to step back and look at the bigger picture. There's hardly enough time to work on the smaller picture. And then you get waylaid by the day-to-day practicalities of it all, like figuring out how to stick the smaller pictures on the wall.

Perhaps the best way to illustrate the mood of the times

is to briefly examine just one aspect of the semantics of the situation. At the time, the 'failings' of many of the second-generation immigrant children within schools was explained by the fact that for them, at home, English was a second language. Now undoubtedly this was true. But the classification was all about defining a problem. It was about finding the negative. However, I would argue that there was another way of looking at it all. All you had to say was not that these children had English as 'a second language', but that they were bilingual. They were six years old and they already spoke two languages. They weren't children who should be looked down on, they were children who should be looked up to. Unfortunately because one of the languages wasn't French, not many people saw just how talented these children were.

My mother's response was somewhat different. She looked out on a classroom full of different races and different cultures and saw not just the problems, but also the possibilities. When she considered the teaching materials available at the time, however, she realised there was a severe mismatch between what was available and what was needed. In particular, she grew concerned that the storybooks she had access to reflected very little of the cultural heritage of the children in her charge.

If I think back to my own time at primary school, I can remember finding in the school library only one book that had a lead character who was not white. It was a book called, and I apologise for this in advance, *Little Black Sambo*. If anything, the story line was more disturbing than the title. If I'm remembering it correctly, Little Black Sambo was a small boy from Africa and he got chased round a tree by a tiger, and then he dissolved into a pool of butter.

But maybe I'm remembering it wrong. Maybe I was too young to understand the sophistication of the plot. Maybe it was really a scathing satire on Britain's failings as a colonial power. Unfortunately, however, I think it was really about a black boy, who got chased round a tree and ended up as a pool of butter.

What was all that about?

In retrospect, the really worrying thing was that the primary school I went to was a good school.

My mother's father was a great storyteller. And so was my mother. Remembering the stories she'd heard as a child, she realised that maybe it was through stories that she could give back to the children she was teaching some of their own heritage that they were missing out on. So she started researching indigenous folk tales. From India. From Pakistan. From China. From Jamaica. From Senegal. From Kenya. From Greece. From Turkey. From Ireland.

And she started storytelling. In schools. In libraries. In parks. Wherever she went, children would gather to listen. The more stories she told, the better she got at it. She learned how to judge the level of an audience. She learned how to choose the right story. She learned how to speed up, or slow down, depending on whether the audience were on the edge of boredom, or the edge of their seats. And she learned what she had known all along. She learned that everyone loves a good story.

Of course, because the stories she told were folk tales, there would often be a moral contained in the narrative. But she knew that children don't listen for the moral, they listen for the story. Show them worlds they've never seen, give them heroes and villains to cheer and hiss, give them adventures and heartbreaks to thrill and move them, and delight them with comic characters that make them laugh, and the listening children will absorb the other messages on a subliminal level that will add to their very core.

That she did a lot of storytelling in parks is also something for which I have great admiration. These were just the neighbourhood parks, filled with neighbourhood kids. And along with the young children who were used to listening to stories, she would frequently be faced with bored teenagers who often saw a sari-clad storyteller in the park as fair game for a heckle or two. But the strange thing is that my mother never got into any real difficulties. Then again, storytelling works on different levels. And while bored teenagers might have long ago outgrown the days when they would listen to a story, they probably still remember those days. Also, even the most jaded of feckless youths know when someone is trying to do something, if not for them, then for their younger brothers and sisters. Especially if they already knew that they were part of a largely marginalised and ignored community.

My mother also developed the art of storytelling for adults. And soon she was speaking at conferences and running workshops on what had, in an increasingly multimedia age, so very nearly become a lost art.

The story I most remember from my mother's time as a storyteller came from India and was called 'The Bharunda Bird'. It was about a beautiful and mythical bird with two heads. It was the most wondrous creature in the land. Although the two heads had two distinct personalities, as their long necks intertwined, they lived in perfect harmony. One would feed the other. One would scratch the other's neck when it needed scratching. Then one day, one of the heads got tired of the other head. It railed against the fact that the other head was always following it around. It despised the fact that the other head knew everything that it was doing. It hated the fact that it couldn't lead its own life. So it came up with a plan. It found some berries that it knew were poisonous and began singing their praises. Then, in a show of fake generosity and kindness, it let the other head eat them first. Then the other head would die. In many ways it was a good plan. But in one crucial way it was a terrible one. That's because while the Bharunda Bird had two heads, it only had one stomach. And so the Bharunda Bird died.

Like I said, my father was a good cook, but he didn't get the chance to do much cooking. When he did, it was the aromas of Ceylon that wafted through the house. One of the dishes I have strongest memories of him preparing was called mallung. It was a very simple vegetable dish made with any green, leafy vegetable, cooked quickly at the last minute, and served immediately.

CABBAGE MALLUNG
SERVES 3

8oz cabbage
½ medium onion, chopped
2 green chillies, finely chopped
oil for frying
½ teaspoon brown mustard seeds
½ teaspoon turmeric
salt, to taste
2 tablespoons desiccated coconut
juice ½ lime

Wash and finely shred the cabbage. Fry the onions and chilli in a little oil. Mix the other ingredients (except the lime) together in bowl. Add to the pan and stir-fry for 2–3 minutes. Remove from heat, squeeze lime juice over and serve.

What I remember most about my father cooking this is not the actual cooking but the preparation. The cooking only took a couple of minutes. The preparation took as long as it took. My father had big, strong fingers. Fingers still stained at the nails by years of smoking Senior Service cigarettes. But fingers which, when he chopped up cabbage for mallung, had the precision and touch of the artist that he was. He would pull the leaves from the cabbage, wash them carefully, then roll several leaves into a tight bunch and hold it together with one strong hand. Then with the largest, sharpest knife in the kitchen he would cut the cabbage into the thinnest of shreds. Not for him any of the showy, blade-wielding trickery of today's TV chefs. No, for him the job had to be done well, done carefully and paying full respect to what you were doing. The dish itself was one of the simplest you could imagine. But the attention he gave to preparing it elevated it into something far more profound.

In many ways I think it was a matter of attitude. And philosophy. I think, by his actions, he was saying that you should give the food you eat the respect it is due. That even the simplest dish, prepared with care, and with love, becomes something beyond the ingredients that made it, and the time it took to cook.

My father thought deeply about things. However, he rarely expressed what he thought directly. No doubt it is there in his paintings. But for me, more importantly, it was there in how he lived his life. How he cooked was just another canvas for him.

I can also remember him saying, 'If you're doing the ironing, do the ironing.' For a very long time I didn't fully understand this. For years, in what I imagined to be my time-poor life, ironing was just a chore that had to be done and got out of the way as quickly as possible. What I think he was getting at is that life is nothing but a collection of moments. And if you don't live each moment as fully as you can, you're missing out on life itself. So if you're doing something, no matter how dull, just do it. Free yourself from judgements about it and the task becomes less of a task. You might even find meaning in the mundane.

He also used to say, 'One plus one equals two minus one.'

But I'm still trying to figure that one out.

For me no serious contemplation of food, family and cultural identity could be complete without the mention of plastic boxes. More specifically, my mother's plastic boxes that live in her fridge and which, throughout my life, have been filled with food and handed out to family and friends at the end of any visit that has involved even the most modest of meals.

There are, of course, many reasons my mother has given over the years to explain her actions.

'You're always so busy, it'll save you cooking when you get home.'

'I've made too much and I'll never eat it all.'

'Just take a little home for [insert name of missing partner, relative or friend who couldn't make the visit] to try.'

'It always tastes better the day after you cook it.'

Naturally, there is also the universal question that in four short words encapsulates so much of the trials and tribulations and responsibilities of being a mother, and which never stops, no matter that your children have long since grown up and moved out, have been through primary, secondary and tertiary education, have found employment and even built reasonably successful careers, have survived the highs and lows of countless relationships but eventually found the right person and settled down, have long got used to having their own bank account, paying their own bills, owning their own home and even knowing where the tap is should there be a burst pipe in the winter and they need to turn the water off at the mains, have had children of their own who haven't yet been taken into care by the local authorities, and have never, ever, in all the years since they've left home, been in any real danger of starving to death.

That question being, 'Are you eating properly?'

I say 'plastic boxes' because that's what they are. We're not talking Tupperware here. We're talking plastic boxes. Any type of plastic box. At any one time, jostling for space in my mother's fridge – the inside of which looks worryingly like an overlit miniature container port – you'll find a recycled Utterly Buttery tub, next to a washed and reused Chinese takeaway container, all sitting on a large white box that once contained ice cream. Alongside them you will find the Tupperware (or the supermarket own-label equivalent), but for some reason actual Tupperware doesn't have the same resonance or meaning as the reincarnated boxes that are working their way through their own karmic life cycles.

Now, while the boxes may not be the star attraction, they are, in their own way, key components in everything that is going on. So while it's the food that we're really interested in as the repository of cultural heritage, it's the hitherto unsung plastic boxes that allow this culinary heritage to be passed on from one generation to the next. If you like, they're the equivalent of those silver-haired ladies who give up their weekends to work at National Trust properties, handing round the laminated sheets of paper that tell you exactly what you're looking at in the room once you've got past remarking upon the size of the fireplaces.

Historically, there is probably a subliminal link between the plastic boxes and the tiffin carrier. The tiffin carrier was, and still is, an integral part of life in the east. It is a collection of pans that can be stacked on top of each other and has a handle that clips over and seals the whole affair. Into each pan a different dish could be placed. It is a way of carrying a full and varied meal to school, to work or to family and friends. A good tiffin carrier is both useful and practical and can be used daily for years. It is, in short, a design classic.

Unfortunately, they've never really caught on in Britain. This, despite the fact that not long ago I spotted a site in Soho that was once a sandwich bar now boasting a place that sold stacks of Indian food in disposable tiffin carriers. It wasn't doing a roaring trade. That's because there still remains in the majority of the British, where their food is concerned, a deeply conservative streak. They don't like their food mucked about with. Hence, for them, curry is a horizontal, not a vertical affair.

Even though the streets of Soho now teem with an indigenous population many of whom are clearly second-generation immigrants, the whole concept of a tiffin carrier just doesn't resonate. For those for whom it does resonate it probably rings bells of the Raj and the Empire, and Helena Bonham Carter in a crinolined and corseted marquee of a frock poncing about in some Merchant-Ivory guff.

If only the people who'd opened the place had talked to me first. I would have soon put them on the right track.

What they needed to do was save their money on the large, gleaming, chiller display cabinets, and instead swanned off to Comet and picked up a job lot of fridges and filled them with ex-Utterly Butterly tubs of home-cooked Indian food. Then they should have staffed the place, not with kids in some Nehru-collared pastiche of Indian attire, but with Asian mothers of a certain age wearing saris and cardigans. Finally a name should have been chosen that would have really hit home. My preference would have been for: 'Are You Eating Properly?'

Then they could have sat back and just counted the money as every second-generation immigrant in central London turned up and tucked in. On second thoughts, the place wouldn't make any money at all. That's because portion-control would be a real problem. Asian mothers of a certain age, wearing saris and cardigans, invariably force more food upon you than you could possibly eat. No matter how adamantly you say, 'No, Mum, that's too much, keep something for yourself,' they will persist in their actions. They will say, 'Don't worry about me, I've got plenty left in the pan.' So you look into the pan and discover not only is there not 'plenty', but what there is in there is far from the choicest cuts of, for instance, the chicken curry in question. 'But, Mum,' you protest, 'you've only got the neck and the elbows in there.' That's when they hit you with the line to which there is no reply:

'But they're the best bits.'

At which point you might as well admit defeat. You come from two different worlds. You deal in two different sets of criteria. You live your lives according to two fundamentally contradictory philosophies. She is a mother. You are a child. And the exchange of a plastic container full of food is a ritual that cuts to the very core of who you both are and how you relate.

In the case of my mother, you can trace the roots of the practice back to her role in her family when she was young. She was the oldest daughter of quite a large brood. As such it would have fallen on her shoulders to help out my grandmother with looking after the younger children. She'd have to make sure that what at times must have been fairly meagre supplies got evenly distributed around all the hungry mouths. And it was a situation made worse by my grandfather's generosity.

In Burma he was a man with a good job and decent pay. He worked hard, lived in a good home, raised a warm and loving family. And the world that he moved through was a sociable and friendly place. Everyone knew you and you knew everyone. The walk home from work was an endless succession of 'Hello, how are you?'s. When the family relocated to London he found the change very difficult. The weather was cold and wet, the atmosphere was dour and depressing, and as you sat on the bus on the interminable journey to the office no one met your eye, let alone said hello.

For a man of his temperament it was all very hard to take. But try as it might, the world he now found himself in couldn't completely crush his spirit. When he passed a fellow immigrant in the street he thought looked as down as he felt, he would engage them in conversation. As is the way in the east, all such encounters would end in an invitation to come back home and have something to eat. Then he would head back to my grandmother with one cloud temporarily removed from his horizon by his act of kindness. He would waltz up to his wife as she stood by the stove and say, 'Edie-girl, there might be one more for dinner.'

That's another great thing about a curry. If you make enough gravy you can always sling in a few extra potatoes and the whole thing will stretch just a little bit further.

In the last year or so, however, I have found myself in a period of transition. My mother left her home of forty years in South London and moved closer to me. Now her health is running into a series of problems that she's finding difficult to shake off. So we seem to have reached the stage where the roles are starting to reverse. Now, when I visit her, I'm the one taking her food in plastic boxes. I'm the one asking, 'Are you eating properly?'

But she's not giving up without a fight. So while I'm giving her plastic boxes of food that I've cooked, she's giving me plastic boxes of food that she's cooked. It doesn't really make a lot of sense. But it means something important. I think it's something to do with love. And our inability to express it in words. Expressing it, however obliquely, in actions, is so much easier.

If I leave her home with one less box than I arrived with, I judge it a success. Not that I'm really complaining, because what she cooks for me always tastes ten times better than the bolognaises and stews I cook for her.

sixteen
A CURRY AFTER WORK

The John Snow is a pub in Soho, central London, where I used to drink. Go and visit it today and it is as unremarkable as a hundred others. When I used to be a customer, almost twenty years ago, it was even less distinguished. It was a down-at-heel boozer with all the charm of a lager-soaked beer mat and a half-eaten packet of pork scratchings. Upstairs at the Snow was even more of a dive.

Hard, then, not to fall in love with the place.

I fell for its charms because, for almost three years, I worked in offices opposite it. This particular advertising agency was my second job, and the one where I first felt that I might actually know what I was doing. The agency didn't do particularly good work, but the people who worked there did have a particularly good time.

Just reeling off the names and I'm back in a world where, at last, I began to feel I fitted in. There was Chris,

Dick, Lynne, Joan, Ruth, Mark, Dave, Keith, Katie, Waudby, Laura, Terrie, Hilary, Billy, Mike, Anne-Marie, Stokesy, Colin and Pickard. Each was a distinct character. All seemed to have personality to spare. Chris was unfeasibly tall and would spend lunchtimes having the San Marco café construct sandwiches for him that almost matched his own height. Dick had a deadpan sense of humour that took no prisoners and he could draw a caricature of you in minutes so accurate that you didn't know whether to laugh or wince. And Pickard was a mad woman from Barnsley who'd somehow escaped south, with a voice as loud as two foghorns and a laugh as dirty as a week down t'pit.

Who these people were matters because work, to my mind, is never really about work. Most people, most of the time, are fairly bored by what they do. Yes, of course, you get interested in it, but you're not really interested in it. It's what you do to make a living. But living is what you do somewhere else. That working takes up such a vast portion of our waking lives is a bizarre anomaly. The way round it is to chisel out activities that make the working day less of a drag. So a chat in the kitchen while you wait for the kettle to boil is, actually, what makes working bearable. As does swearing at the photocopier, as it annoyingly winks at you the hieroglyphic message to 'add toner' when you haven't the faintest idea where the toner is stored, nor would you be able to 'add' it even if you did. And, of course, there is office gossip. Where would we be without office gossip? Well, we'd be in offices devoid of almost all distraction, which would leave us vast, empty, filing cabinets of time in which to contemplate the utter banal meaninglessness of what we actually did all day.

Upstairs at the Snow was where the gossip got really good. It was all regurgitated and picked over round two battered pool tables, while the wall-mounted jukebox by the window endlessly repeated UB40s 'Rat In Mi Kitchen'. The pub, in retrospect, had absolutely nothing to recommend it. Upstairs had even less. But it was across the road. And going there had the air about it of playing football with your mates after school before you had to go home and do your homework.

After a couple of hours of beer and pool and who's sleeping with, or not sleeping with, or totally pissed off with, whom, we'd start to get hungry. The lido of beer in your belly would cry out to be soaked up. Invariably it would be Dick who would propose the next stage of the evening.

'Who fancies going to the Maharini for a curry?'

We all did, because if we didn't we'd have to go home. And it's not as if there was anything decent on the telly.

If the John Snow could have been any one of a hundred pubs, then the Maharini in Wardour Street could have been any one of a thousand Indian restaurants. It was all low lighting, flock wallpaper and a decidedly garish picture of the Taj Mahal on the wall, just in case you were so far gone by the time you staggered in that you forgot what type of restaurant this was and ordered a pizza. I won't tell you what was on the menu as you probably already know. You probably also know what you'd order if you wandered in and pulled up a chair.

Everyone always had what they always had. Me, I had a meat biriani and a raita, Lynne would have a chicken madras and a naan, and Dick would have meat vindaloo, tarka daal and Bombay potato. And we'd all have a beer. Or three. The first would be necked down while we demolished a crumbling tower of poppadoms whose shattered floors would be dipped into the shiny silver carousel of pickles and chutneys. Beer number two would be called for as the food arrived. And beer three, often just a half, would be a way of fending off the sad inevitability of having to finally call it a night.

When it was all over we would troop out of the narrow corridor of a room, invariably banging our chairs into those of the diners behind us. Then would come the affectionate sarcasms of pavement farewells that lingered on so long that an onlooker would never have guessed that we'd all be together again, back at work, the next morning, or the next Monday.

I realise that just as the pub and the restaurant were both unremarkable, so was this whole 'going for a curry' experience. Up and down the country, in countless other Taj Mahals or Jewel In The Crowns or Curry Cabins, similar scenes were no doubt being played out. But for me this common currency was being spent in an entirely new way. For me, up until then, curry had been about family. Here, in the cramped confines of the Maharini in Wardour Street, curry had become about friends. It had become a social space in which to laugh and joke and whinge and argue and flirt and tease and, when the bill eventually came, to get annoyed with the one person in the party (and there is always one) who insists on paying only for precisely what they had eaten. And as you walk home in a haze of happiness you realise that you've eaten more than you should, paid less than you feared and enjoyed yourself more than the simple ingredients of the evening had any right to provide.

But maybe I'm missing the point by saying that for me curry had always been about family, and here it was about friends. Maybe the point is that we live in a world where, for many people, for much of the time, family doesn't mean what it used to. We no longer operate in emotionally and geographically tight-knit units based on kinship. The nuclear family has exploded and we're all living with the fallout. One of the strategies we've developed to survive is, perhaps, that we've turned friends into 'family'. If we have done that, then maybe part of the secret of the success of Indian restaurants in Britain is that they function as the dining room in which these new 'families' that we've chosen to belong to can sit down together and eat.

So maybe curry in a restaurant is still about family. It's just that the nature of the family has changed.

I'm thinking that when my mother eventually gives up the ghost, maybe I'll suggest to my brother we go in for an alternative to the traditional wooden coffin. I mean, there must be a manufacturer out there who makes very large plastic boxes. And when you think about it, it would be an eminently practical way of going about things. After all, the great thing about a plastic box is that it is reusable. You just have to make sure it's got a resealable lid.

Think of the advantages. Manufacture the thing with just the right degree of translucency and all the mourners at the funeral would be able to get a not-too-disturbingly detailed glimpse of the deceased towards which they could focus their thoughts. The few times I've been to a funeral I've found myself staring at a wooden box, trying to think about the person inside. I mean, work with me on this one, but aren't you there to say goodbye to the person, not the coffin?

If the plastic box was reusable, just consider the environmental benefits. After my mother's funeral we could wash it out and keep it until the next time. And in between uses it could be pressed into service as storage. Maybe for clothes. Or shoes. Or even bulk purchases of rice. Anyway, seeing as my mother loves trees, why should one get cut down just to build a box for her to get sent off in?

But the main reason for doing it would be, in my mother's case, that it was appropriate. Also it would make me, and my brother, and all the people who knew and loved her, laugh. No doubt it will be a point in our lives when we could do with a little laughter.

OK, I admit, I've probably gone a bit far. So let's just shelve the idea of the plastic coffin. Instead, come the day, maybe all I'll do is cook a vast pot of one of my mother's favourite curries, and as the mourners take their leave I'll press upon them individual plastic boxes of food for them to eat when they get back home. And I'll bid them farewell with a message from my mother that I know will strike a chord.

'Are you eating properly?'

I've just rung my mum and asked her what food she wants served at her funeral. She said that she hadn't really thought about it. I say what about kyaukswe? She says no, that will only splash all over everyone's best clothes. I say she may well have a point. She says she'll think about what to serve. And I say OK and hang up the phone.

But you and me both know I'm going to cook kyaukswe. And if it splashes on the clothes, it splashes on the clothes. Think of it as my family's equivalent of that old Jewish custom where people rip their clothes as a way of expressing their grief. Only, as a way of expressing grief, eating a bowl of kyaukswe has a hell of a lot more to be said for it than ripping your clothes.

And I have the beautiful vision in my mind of mourners at the wake turning to each other, in their emotionally bereft state, and saying, 'Needs more lemon.'

When I was in my mid-twenties I went to work in Singapore. I went because I needed to move on from the job I had at the time, and because getting paid to live somewhere exotic seemed too good an opportunity to miss. But I mainly went because I was running away from a broken heart. I know that packing up house and home, saying goodbye to friends and family and relocating halfway around the globe is a bit of an extreme reaction to the collapse of a romance but, as they say in the movies, it seemed a good idea at the time. Anyway, I reckon that if in the course of your life you don't have at least one extreme reaction to some affair of the heart that's hit the pavement like a tomato chucked from the top of a tower block, then you haven't really lived.

In the end I only stayed in Singapore for ten months out of a two-year contract, mainly because I found myself with less responsibility than I had in London. And my broken heart had mended. What I do remember most distinctly was how strange, yet how natural, it felt to live and work in a place where white faces weren't in the majority. Of course, I had the advantage of coming into the country as a member of a relatively highly paid, expatriate professional elite. But I don't think that was the only reason I felt a type of ease in Singapore that I'd rarely felt in London.

On the way home I had planned to go to Burma and visit the places where my mother grew up. But I couldn't get in. At the time, student unrest had kicked off in Rangoon. When I applied for my visa I was turned down. My passport said that I was a copywriter and that was interpreted by the official as a writer. Writer meant journalist. And journalist meant trouble.

Instead I went home via Sri Lanka, where I stopped over for little more than a day. I stayed in a hotel near the airport and my uncle, my father's brother, drove out from Colombo to pick me up and take me out to lunch. He took me to a restaurant that was little more than a canteen where they served food on banana leaves and offered customers five different types of crab curry. Having just decamped from Singapore, I thought that I'd already had as good a crab curry as it was possible to get. But I was wrong. The crab curry in Sri Lanka was from another planet. The fact that you had to engage the crab in hand-to-claw combat just to get to the meat made the spoils of war all the more prized.

My uncle was my father's younger brother, and when my father had gone off to England to find a new life, he had stayed behind to fight it out at home. And he had done spectacularly well. Starting off from humble origins he had climbed his way to the highest echelons of the legal profession. He had done it with a smile never far from his lips, and a keen interest in helping those less fortunate than himself. He possessed that rare combination of blessings of being both well respected and well liked.

As his life was in Sri Lanka, and ours was in the UK, we didn't get to see him very often. But on the rare occasions when he did get together with my father, you could see in their eyes that there was a bond between them that would never be broken.

Between mouthfuls of crab curry that day, I tried out a couple of tentative questions about the memories he had about growing up with my dad. He told me about the time when he was still quite small when their own father got the two of them and their sister up very early one morning and they set off to walk several miles to try to enrol in a particular school. When they got there, because their father didn't have enough money, they were turned away and had to walk all the way back home. Fifty years on, for my uncle, now a QC, the indignity of the experience still burned somewhere down in the back of his psyche.

So I asked my uncle if they were poor. He said that he didn't think so at the time, but that he remembered waking up one night to find his father sitting by a lidded pot of rice. In his hands was a large stick of wood. When he asked his father what the stick was for, he said it was to whack the big rat that lived in the rafters who would come down in the night to try to steal the rice. And it was rice they couldn't afford to lose.

But beyond that he didn't really say much. I suppose I didn't know him well enough to ask the right questions. And I have the feeling that even if I had asked the right questions, he, for his own reasons, probably wouldn't have answered.

When I got back to London I found it all a considerable shock to the system. Mind you, I did hit town just as the Christmas party season was in full swing. When you've just spent the best part of a year among the elegance and dignity of the people of Southeast Asia, a drunken Friday night after work in a pub, up in Soho, takes some getting used to.

At first I thought it was jet lag. But then I realised there are lots of other lags out there that you can suffer from when you've just flown halfway round the world.

sixteen
and a half
A BRIEF HISTORY OF CURRY
IN BRITAIN: A POSTSCRIPT

I know I said I'd finished my brief history, but if I left it where I did I would be doing the industry a disservice. That's because in the early 1980s the Indian restaurant trade did what it was good at. It evolved. The evolution was fuelled by the convergence of three main factors. First there was the emergence of restaurateurs who weren't satisfied with the limited, though successful, horizons of the curry houses. Second, among these same entrepreneurs, there was a frustration with the limited style of cooking that Indian restaurants were serving. India offers a vast range of diverse and delicious regional cuisines – the sauce-based fast food of the standard curry house came nowhere near doing it anything like justice. The third factor was, of course, Mrs Thatcher.

Not that she had anything to do with cooking curry, or even eating it, but she did help create the economic climate in which a new breed of Indian restaurants became a viable option. Essentially, in the economic boom years of early Thatcherism, money – earning it, having it and spending it – became OK. It stopped being somewhat vulgar. Or, as Gordon Gekko so aptly put it in the movie *Wall Street*, greed was good. And Harry Enfield's character Loadsamoney – a wodge-waving plasterer – might have started out as a parody, but within a couple of outings had turned into a role model.

Given this climate it's little wonder that eating out suddenly wasn't just about eating out. It became less about consumption and more about conspicuous consumption. Eating in restaurants, especially up-market expensive ones, became the newest way for self-definition in a society where consumerism ruled supreme.

What this meant for restaurants was that, get the formula right, and they could turn from businesses into goldmines. After all, if your lunchtime customers were sticking it all on expenses anyway, then how closely were they going to look at the bill? Indeed, if decidedly not looking at the bill became a badge of financial machismo, then weren't you shifting from the business of serving food to the business of printing money?

The entrepreneurs at the cutting edge of Indian cooking noted the new atmosphere and decided that they too wanted a slice of the gulab jam. The first restaurant to make the break was the Bombay Brasserie, set up in December 1982 by

Camellia Panjabi. It opened in the large and airy, refurbished breakfast room of the previously unkempt Bailey's Hotel. The look of the place was like something out of *The Far Pavilions* – all cane peacock chairs, pink and gold plaster-work, potted palms and Parsi paintings. The food was authentic, regional, and served not in communal curry-house dishes but already plated-up, just like in a high-class French restaurant. Four days after it opened, Fay Maschler, the country's leading restaurant critic, walked in and sat down. Born in India herself, she liked what she saw. Even more importantly, she liked what she ate. Hence a rave review. And the next stage of curry in Britain was off and running.

In 1984 Amin Ali opened the Red Fort in Soho. Its attitude to the food it served echoed that of the Bombay Brasserie. This too was to be a dining experience, not a place to stagger into after the pubs had chucked out. The decor of the place, however, moved things on. The themes may have been Indian, but it wasn't steeped in nostalgia for an idealised version of the Raj. It was modern, it was stylish, and it had the confidence not to hark back to the days of colonialism in order to make the clientele it was aiming for feel at ease. On top of all that, Ali pulled the masterstroke of hiring a PR man to get the restaurant written about, and talked about, in all the right places. And by all the right people. That the ploy worked can be gauged by the list of movers and shakers and politicians who would regularly eat at the Red Fort.

Since the early 1980s upmarket Indian restaurants have made steady advances. Allied to this has been the growth in the number of establishments offering regional cuisine. And other individuals have made names for themselves. Cyrus Todiwala opened Cafe Spice Namaste. Iqbal Wahhab – the Red Fort PR man – opened the Cinnamon Club. And Namita and Camellia Panjabi launched the very popular Masala Zone, which offered high-quality Indian street food at curry-house prices.

The real recognition that Indian cooking had stepped up into another league came in 2001. That's when the chef Atul Kochar, at the restaurant Tamarind in Chelsea, won a Michelin star. This was soon followed by a similar award for Vineet Bhatia's restaurant Zaika, also in Chelsea.

With the official culinary seal of approval of a Michelin star, the curry had finally arrived at the top table. It was all a very long way from flock wallpaper, wipe-clean menus and, 'Oh, I'll have what I always have, and could we get some more poppadoms and who wants another lager?'

But.

But, admirable though the move into higher quality, more authentic and diversely delicious regional variations of cooking undoubtedly is, I can't help feeling that these new restaurants are somewhat peripheral to Britain's love affair with curry. Of course, the food you get in these places is far, far better than the standard curry-house fare. And of course the people doing the cooking are not just cooks, but bona fide chefs with both skills and knowledge to match those that can be found in any haute cuisine establishment. It's just that to my way of thinking they are, somewhat, missing the point. Or maybe it's just that they are pursuing a completely different point.

The best of these places purposely set out to establish themselves as not just outstanding Indian restaurants, but as outstanding restaurants. They wanted to be mentioned in the same breath as any other of the upmarket, fine dining experiences that could be had in London. And they have succeeded. But, in doing so, they have become just another fine dining experience.

The bog-standard curry house, on the other hand, offers so much less. But somehow you come away from eating at one of them with so much more. And I'm not just talking about the cash in your wallet. That's because 'going for a curry' has achieved the thing that so rarely happens in this world. And the thing that all great art aspires to. It transcends. It transcends the fairly humble nature of the components that comprise it and somehow moves the experience to a higher level. Just as Debussy's *Clair de Lune* is more than a few notes tinkled on a piano, and a Shakespeare sonnet is more than some words on a page, and a Thierry Henry goal is more than a bloke with a football having a kick-about with his mates, 'going for a curry' is far more than a pile of poppadoms, a korma and a pint of lager. That it has achieved this more through a combination of luck and circumstance than by design is all part of its glory.

Things rarely become part of the culture. And when they do they should be treated with respect. But, obviously, not too much respect as we are just talking about food here. And, anyway, when it comes to curry, 'respect' is completely the wrong word. 'Love' is the word. People love curry. And who can blame them?

* * *

Mind you, I may well have a personal bias against the new breed of upmarket Indian restaurants. That's because I was, in all likelihood, one of the first people to be banned from one of them.

My first ever full-time job was at a small advertising agency in Soho back in 1984. The agency was initially sited in a back alley called Diadem Court, opposite a DHSS office that seemed to cater for a somewhat alcoholically dishevelled clientele. As the agency was doing well, it soon realised that having to steer its own smartly suited clients past those of the place opposite probably didn't create the best impression. At the earliest possible opportunity the company decided to decamp round the corner onto Dean Street. So, one Saturday, everyone went in to help with the move and to make sure that all their stuff ended up in the right place.

By late afternoon, when the move was finished, the MD decided to thank everyone for their help by taking them out to the Nelly Dean pub for a drink or two. After that, he was going to stand us all dinner at the fancy new restaurant that had just opened next to what were now our new offices. It was a restaurant called the Red Fort.

I won't go into the details of our meal, but at the end of it we were asked never to come back. It's not that anyone was abusive, it's just that a couple of our party were some-what the worse for wear. No, that's not a fair description, they were, actually, to quote a phrase much used at the time, 'as pissed as a fart'. Hence they were a tad more raucous than was strictly called for. Which made us, somewhat ironically, just the kind of alcoholically dishevelled clientele that the Red Fort thought probably didn't create the best impression with its own smartly suited clients. So we were banned. All of us. Including me.

Which was a shame as the food was excellent.

About seventeen years later I did go back to the Red Fort. But luckily by then I had changed my hair, so no one recognised me.

seventeen

'THE ARENA OF FOOD'

A few years after I'd given up actively seeking work in advertising – because I was making enough money from writing books and because I'd really had enough of talking bollocks every day – I got a phone call from a producer of TV commercials with whom I'd once worked. Her name was Helen and she had a proposition. An advertising agency had approached her because she had a very talented Asian director on her books, and this agency needed someone to direct some commercials that BT were planning to run on one of the Hindi satellite TV channels.

She had the Asian director. Now what the advertising agency needed was an Asian copywriter. Someone who was part of the 'Asian community'. Well, I may well have been Asian, or at very least of Asian descent, but in so many ways I wasn't part of the mythical 'Asian community'. I explained this to Helen. But she talked me round.

I ended up in a meeting with a sharply suited and smooth talking ad-man. Unfortunately, I found it worryingly easy to start spouting the strategically astute, pseudo-logical and post-rationalised ramblings that once comprised a major part of my working day. I even found myself using the word 'rationale'. It's long been my belief that should you ever find yourself using the word 'rationale' in a conversation, it's time to go home.

As we walked down the street after the meeting, Helen turned to me and said, 'You don't really want to do it, do you?' I ummed and ahhed and didn't really commit myself. But as we reached the corner where we would go our separate ways, I turned to her and said that she was right, and that I didn't want to slip back into a world I had only just escaped.

Back at home that night, I felt bad about my decision. So I rang Helen and told her that even though I really didn't want to get involved, I'd write up my 'rationale' of what BT should do, come up with a couple of scripts to show how the thing could work, and then send them over to her and she could use them however she liked. If it helped get her director some work, then that would be great.

A week later she rang up and said that BT had bought the whole package and they wanted to meet the team that had come up with the work.

In the end I wrote about twenty scripts and was involved in shooting the three of them that got made. The commercials were filmed in Hindi. I don't speak Hindi. So I'd write the commercials in English, then they'd get presented to the advertising agency. If they liked them, they'd get presented to BT. If BT liked them, the agency would take them away and get them translated into Hindi.

As for the director, who had the serious task of coaxing fine and nuanced performances from his carefully chosen cast, well, he too was a second-generation immigrant. He understood Hindi but he wasn't fluent in it. So there we'd be on set, me the writer, him the director (along with the producer, the soundman and the entire rest of the English-speaking crew), trying to film commercials that would really strike a chord with the Hindi-speaking Indian community in Britain, when none of us had any real idea what the actors were saying.

I tell you all this as a way of illustrating just how convolutedly odd this whole second-generation business can be.

The other reason I'm setting down all this BT shenanigans is this: the way I convinced both the advertising agency and BT that I was au fait with the Asian 'experience' in Britain was that I sold them a campaign that was all about family. And food. I think I may have even used in the presentation the following rationale: 'At the core of any immigrant experience is the issue of family. And for any immigrant family the issues to do with family, and indeed identity (both personal and cultural), are often explored in the Arena of Food.'

Arena of Food? What on earth was I on about?

The commercials featured a typical Asian family. The father owned a corner shop, the son was training to be a doctor, the daughter was heading for an unhappy arranged marriage, and whenever the mother spoke she wobbled her head from side to side.

Oh come on, get a grip, the commercials were nothing like that. And BT would have, rightly, kicked them out the door if they were. So even in the world of commerce, things have moved on.

In the first commercial the mother is on the phone, and the father chips in comments as he constructs a beautiful sandwich of roast chicken, salad and mayonnaise. At the end of the commercial he bites into his masterpiece, finds it lacking something, then solves the evident flavour problem by reaching for the lime pickle jar.

So there you have it. The whole history of Asians in Britain encapsulated in a forty-second commercial. Namely, yeah of course we'll go in for all that assimilation and integration stuff, but, let's be honest here, the food is a bit on the dull side. Food, of course, being a metaphor for so much more.

In the second commercial the son comes home with tales of some minor success and the mother's immediately on the phone talking up his achievements. Simultaneously, she's dishing up a mountain of rice and curry in front of him 'to keep his strength up'.

In the third commercial the daughter rings her mum, bemoaning the despair of splitting up with her latest boyfriend. While the mother comforts her sobbing daughter, she asks the inevitable 'are you eating properly?' question. The daughter says she's lost her appetite. But by the end of the commercial, certain appetites seem to be making a comeback as she opens the door to discover a leather-clad, drop-dead-gorgeous pizza delivery man.

I must admit I'm quite proud of those commercials. They are decently written, well directed and beautifully acted. But I've got no idea what anyone is saying. Because I don't speak Hindi.

Luckily, on the set of the commercials I managed to cover up my lack of language skills by encouragingly saying of each take: 'It's very good, but, you know, everything can be improved.' I got away with it for a while. Then, uncertain about a slight change to the nuance of a line she was speaking, the actress playing the mother turned to me and asked me what I thought. In Hindi.

Somewhat shamefacedly I had to admit my predicament. Yes, I did write this commercial. Yes, I am judging your performance. No, I don't have any idea what you're saying.

The actress, to my great relief, was not at all thrown. She just said, 'Oh, don't worry. Explain it to me in English, and I'll act it in Hindi.' And she did. Beautifully.

The next day, as we sat down together to eat lunch from the location catering truck, I apologised again to Lalita – the actress – for my ignorance. She laughed off my discomfort. As is common on these occasions, we got talking about the food that was on offer. Somewhat bravely, given the ethnicity of the cast, the catering company had done a curry. Thankfully, commercial catering has moved on a long way from my days back at school, and the people doing the location food weren't just caterers but extremely talented cooks.

I turned the conversation to the fact that I was thinking about writing about the Asian experience of food and family. Once she heard this, Lalita was off and running. She knew more about Indian food than anyone I had ever met. She also totally understood the whole food-family-identity thing. For instance, she told me about how in certain communities back in India, families would be so protective of their recipes that when a daughter married into another family she wasn't allowed to take the secrets with her, because then they would be available to anyone in her new family. She also told me that she had in her possession a very old recipe book, in an almost forgotten language, from a Mughal court, that she was in the process of translating.

It was all incredibly fascinating. So fascinating, in fact, that I said to her that she should write a cookery book of her own. Somewhat modestly, she admitted that she had already. 'What's it called?' I asked. 'I'd love to get a copy.'

'Oh,' she said, 'I don't think you can get it any more. It was called *Indian Cooking*. I did it for Marks & Spencer's.'

That evening I went home and dug out my copy of the book. Lalita's name was proudly emblazoned on the front cover. It had first been published in 1981. My copy was a sixth impression, from 1982. That means that it did so well in the space of a single year back in the 1980s that it outsold its print run six times. And it was the very book that I had tried to make a curry from, until I baulked at the time it would take, the day I had come back from aisle seven of the Harringey branch of Sainsbury's.

* * *

I started out this book as an exploration of something I had lost. I wasn't really sure what precisely it was, but I did know that it was something, no matter how intangible, of great value. Food, the food my mother cooked, the food I had grown up eating, the food I didn't know how to cook for my own children, was the way in.

Identity is always a big issue with second-generation immigrants. Do you belong to the world your parents came from? Or are you really a product of the world you were born into and grew up in? Or is it both? And if it is both, then what is the balance between the two worlds?

I'm not sure that I've ended up with a definitive answer to any of these questions. But then again I'm not sure that definitive answers actually exist. In many ways all I've done is tip up a box of photographs onto a table and picked up and pondered the ones that have struck me as the most interesting. Another person, looking at the same array of images, may have chosen a completely different selection. And who's to say that their choices would be any less valid than mine?

As for what it is to be an immigrant, the thought that strikes me is that if the past really is another country, then we are all immigrants. And the place that we are immigrants from is that past. And the place we have migrated to is the world around us that we live in each day of our lives.

Maybe even trying to define your identity is a futile task. That's because identity is, in fact, a fluid conversation between the past, the present and the future. And how we conduct that conversation can vary from day to day.

The only important thing is to keep the conversation going.

ACKNOWLEDGEMENTS

The family history in this book obviously came from my family. The other historical information was drawn from many other sources. Accordingly, if you want a far better history of curry in Britain than mine, I would like to recommend both *Star Of India: The Spicy Adventures of Curry* by Jo Monroe (John Wiley and Sons Ltd, Chichester 2005), and *Curry: The Story of the Nation's Favourite Dish* by Shrabani Basu (Sutton Publishing, Stroud 2003). Much of the information on the early Portuguese explorers was drawn from a fantastic book by Ronald Watkins called *Unknown Seas: How Vasco da Gama Opened the East* (John Murray, London 2005). I sincerely recommend that you track down a copy and read it.

I must also mention a book that is most precious to me – *The Spice Of Happiness*, by my aunt, Eileen Candappa, and by Harry Haas, which was published by the People's Organization for Development, Import and Export (PODIE, 1982). And then there is the book that crops up at the start and the finish of my own by the wonderful Lalita Ahmed – *Indian Cooking* – written for the St Michael Cookery Library (Octopus Books, London 1981).

The following are other books that provided background research and many delicious diversions:

A Historical Dictionary of Indian Food, K.T. Achaya (Oxford University Press, New Delhi 1982)

Curries and Bugles: A Memoir and Cookbook of the British Raj, Jennifer Brennan (Periplus Editions, Hong Kong 2000)

Anglo-Indian Food and Customs, Patricia Brown (Penguin Books India, New Delhi 1998)

The Spice Routes, Chris and Carolyn Caldicott (Frances Lincoln, London 2001)

Flavours of Burma, Susan Chan (Hippocrene Books, New York 2005)

Pat Chapman's Taste of the Raj, Pat Chapman (Hodder & Stoughton, London 1997)

Sri Lankan Flavours, Channa Dassanayaka (Hardie Grant Books, Victoria 2003)

A Taste of India, Madhur Jaffrey (Pavilion Books Ltd, London 1985)

Madhur Jaffrey's Ultimate Curry Bible, Madhur Jaffrey (Ebury Press, London 2003)

Asians in Britain, Rozina Visram (Pluto Press, London 2002)

Leith's Indian and Sri Lankan Cookery, Priya Wickramasinghe (Bloomsbury, London 1997)

Bloody Foreigners: The Story of Immigration to Britain, Robert Winder (Abacus, London 2004)

The Best of Sainsbury's Oriental Cooking (Cathay Books, London 1987)

ABOUT THE AUTHOR

On the whole he's quite a private person. So he's a little surprised that he's written a book that reveals so much. But seeing as he's gone down that road he might as well fill in the bits of the picture that are missing. His favourite film is *Lawrence of Arabia*; his hair, when it grows, goes curly so he tries to keep it short; and he has a weakness for gadgets that he never really figures out how to use. He likes Rothko, Raymond Carver and *You To Me Are Everything* by The Real Thing. Secretly, he thinks he's quite good at dancing, but worries that he's not. And his favourite animal is the slow loris. Mainly because of its name.